ALEXANDER
THE GREAT

To Richard, who believes Alexander was the greatest demon.

First published in Great Britain 2011 by Walker Books Ltd, 87 Vauxhall Walk, London SE11 5HJ.
This edition published 2012

2 4 6 8 10 9 7 5 3 1

Text © 2011 by Jamila Gavin • Illustration © 2011 by David Parkins

The right of Jamila Gavin and David Parkins to be identified as author and illustrator respectively of this work has been asserted by them in accordance with the Copyright, Designs and Patents Act 1988

This book has been typeset in Monotype Centaur. • Printed in China

Hardback ISBN 978-0-7445-8627-5 • eBook ISBN: 978-1-4063-3915-4

www.walker.co.uk

JAMILA GAVIN

ALEXANDER
THE GREAT

MAN, MYTH OR MONSTER?

Illustrated by DAVID PARKINS

WALKER
BOOKS

CONTENTS

MAP OF ALEXANDER'S EMPIRE 6

1. THE MAKING OF A HERO 11

2. ALEXANDER, THE EMPEROR 22
    The White Stag

3. THE CONQUEST BEGINS 30
    The Story of Achilles

4. TROY 36
    Achilles' Destiny

5. PERSIA: ON ENEMY SOIL 45

6. "LORD OF ALL ASIA" 55
    Artemis and Orion
    The Legend of Gordius

7. THE BATTLE OF ISSUS 70

8. THE SIEGE OF TYRE 78
    The Twelve Labours of Heracles
    The Ambrosial Rocks

9. INTO EGYPT 88
    Osiris and Isis

10. CROSSING THE TIGRIS 102

11. THE BATTLE OF GAUGAMELA 108
    Alexander the Demon

12. BABYLON 121
     Belshazzar's Feast

13. ON THE PERSIAN THRONE 127
     Gilgamesh, the Warrior who Didn't Want to Die

14. PERSEPOLIS 140

15. THE DEATH OF DARIUS 148

16. SAMARKAND 156
     Sohrab and Rostam

17. IN THE FOOTSTEPS OF DIONYSUS 166

18. INDIA 181
     The Hatred that Led to War

19. TO THE ENDS OF THE EARTH 190

20. THE JOURNEY BACK 203

21. THE RETURN TO PERSIA 213
     The Story of Daedalus and Icarus

22. DEATH 222
     Alexander's Hand

     EPILOGUE 233

     CHRONOLOGY 235

     INDEX 236

     ACKNOWLEDGEMENTS 240

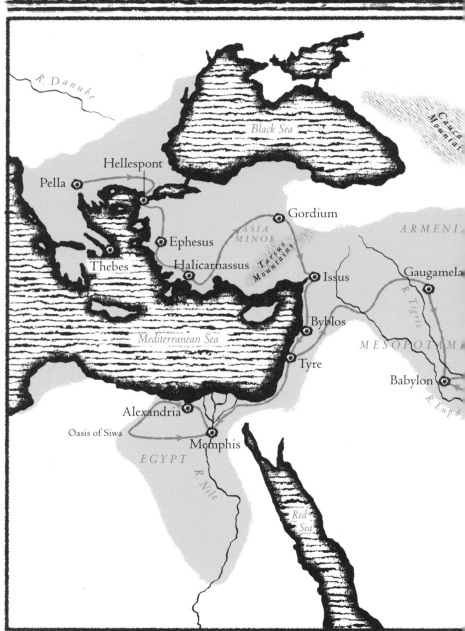

R. Danube

Black Sea

Hellespont

Pella

Gordium

ASIA MINOR

ARMENI

Ephesus

Thebes

Halicarnassus

Tarsus Mountains

Issus

Gaugamela

R. Tigris

MESOPOTAMI

Mediterranean Sea

Byblos

Tyre

Babylon

R. Euph.

Alexandria

Oasis of Siwa

Memphis

EGYPT

R. Nile

Red Sea

Cauca Mountai

Major city
City founded by Alexander
Full extent of Alexander's empire
Principal mountains
Desert

Aral Sea

R. Oxus

Alexandria

Samarkand

SOGDIANA

BACTRIA

Alexandria

Hecatompylus

Bactra

Nysa

Taxila

Alexandria

Caspian Gates

Alexandria

Alexandria

Ecbatana

PARTHIA

Alexandria

Hindu Kush

Alexandria

Bucephala

Jelhum

R. Hydaspes

Alexandria

Alexandria

Alexandria

Alexandria

Alexandria

PERSIA

Persepolis

Alexandria

Alexandria

R. Indus

GEDROSIA

Alexandria

Alexandria

Persian Gulf

Alexandria

Patalla

INDIA

Indian Ocean

Caspian Sea

I believe that, in those times,
no nation, no city, no single person
was beyond the sound of Alexander's name.
Never, in all the world, has there been another like him.
ARRIAN: *THE CAMPAIGNS OF ALEXANDER*

CHAPTER ONE

THE MAKING OF A HERO

Come, come! Gather round and give ear to these tales of Alexander who set out to conquer the world, for they are replete with tears and heroism, defeats and victories, treachery and loyalty, love and passion. He brought terror to his enemies and glory to his followers.

Like Heracles, Alexander was seen as a man in life, a god in death, a being apart, a hero standing between god and human, suffering everything that a man can suffer, testing himself to the limit, overcoming his enemies, enduring his labours in a ceaseless battle with death. He wandered over earth and oceans, experiencing great suffering, but his bravery triumphed, and his many daring exploits were beyond compare. Some said he was the bravest, some said he was the cleverest, some the wiliest, and some the handsomest. Many said that he was the most cruel, and the biggest vandal of all time, and called him Alexander the Damned. But others said he was Alexander the Great. The Greatest.

He was a destroyer of enemies, a builder of cities; who crossed raging rivers and blazing deserts; who flew like an eagle and fought like a lion; who descended to the bottom of the seas in a glass chest to gaze upon a monstrous fish, and was carried high up into the heavens in a flying machine pulled by griffins so that he might map out the world; who encountered amazons and listened to trees with human voices; who fought the horse-riding archers of Bactria and Scythia, and the elephant armies of India.

Give ear to these stories of Alexander, Iskander, Ishkander, Iskindar or Skander; who, on his mighty horse, Bucephalus, was feared by his enemies as the two-horned devil, but revered by his followers as son of Zeus, the greatest by far of the great men on earth.

Who was this Alexander? Was he a myth, a god or a man?

They say he was related to Achilles, to Helen of Troy, to Heracles, and a brother of the god Dionysus, and even that he was the son of Zeus; that his birth was miraculous – not of his human father, Philip, but of Zeus himself. It is said that the day Alexander was born, the temple to Artemis in Ephesus burnt to the ground – an omen prophesying that one day the whole of Asia would burn.

Who can say? All we really know is that Alexander was born in 356 BC, that his mother was the wild, headstrong, scheming Queen Olympias, and his father King Philip II of Macedonia.

Philip was a masterful king and warrior who routed the Greeks and, after the Battle of Chaeronea in 338 BC, became ruler of all the Greek territories including Athens. There was only one power greater than his:

the Persian Empire of Cyrus, Xerxes and Darius.

Alexander was always destined to be king; "But remember, my boy," Philip told his son, "to be an emperor, you must also be a god."

Alexander thought a lot about God, and being a god – but above all, he was a boy who wanted to be a hero.

Do you know what it takes to be a Greek hero? Let me list the qualities!

A hero must be handsome.

Alexander was handsome. Look at the statues, mosaics and reliefs if you don't believe me. Alexander was as wonderfully handsome as the god Apollo. He was not tall, but he had a strong, muscular, athletic body, a noble head with long flowing locks, a broad brow, a straight nose and, most mesmerizing of all, some reported, one eye which was blue, the other black. It was said that even his breath and his body were as fragrant as lilies.

A hero must be tough and fleet of foot.

Just as well that he had a tough and strict disciplinarian for a teacher, Leonidas. Who among you could put up with the harsh regime Alexander endured? He was woken before dawn each day. Instead of breakfast, he had to walk for miles. When he returned, he had studies all day in literature, science and gymnastics, and finally got breakfast at dinner time. Leonidas even rummaged through Alexander's belongings to make sure his mother hadn't smuggled in any forbidden treats for him.

A hero must be educated.

Philip made sure his son was trained in all the skills of kingship, not just to be tough and skilled in warfare, but to be a ruler who could administer justice, be a leader of men and respect learning. Although Philip was Macedonian, it was Greek learning and culture which was valued above all, and was a necessity for any educated man. So there was no question that Alexander must be educated as a Greek. Alexander learned to admire the plays of Euripides and Aeschylus, he knew the histories of Herodotus, and he loved music and poetry. Most of all he loved Homer's *Iliad*, written a thousand years before Alexander was born; the story about the war between the Greeks and the Trojans. Throughout his life, Alexander was never without a copy of the *Iliad*. He loved reading about the battles, the weapons, the stories of the gods and, above all, about the extraordinary god-hero, Achilles. For Alexander, Achilles was the hero of all heroes, the man he wanted to be.

> *Achilles, son of Peleus, the swift-footed, the mightiest of warriors; as in the still hours of night Hesper goes forth among the host of stars, the fairest light of heaven, so brightly shone, brandished in his right hand, the spear's keen blade.*

Achilles was part man, part mortal. He had been educated to the highest degree; instructed by Chiron, the centaur, and by Phoenix, King of the Dolopes, in the arts of warfare, literature and oratory.

Achilles personified the hero, who preferred to die gloriously in battle, with a fearsome reputation that would live for ever, rather than withdraw to the safety of a quiet life, and die in his bed, unknown. This too, was Alexander's ambition.

The best teachers were summoned to educate the young prince. The great Aristotle taught him philosophy, biology, botany and political science, and gave him a deep interest in medicine. At an early age, he showed signs of being precociously clever, always asking questions about warfare, strategy and weapons. He loved music and theatre. He played the lyre. Once he asked his music teacher why it mattered what string he played. The teacher replied, "It doesn't matter if you want to be a king, but it does matter if you want to be a musician."

A hero must be hospitable, compassionate, have respect for the gods and love his mother.

Alexander had all those qualities. He was respectful of women, and was especially close to his mother, Olympias. But she was so full of ambition, always scheming on behalf of her son, always meddling and watching over him, that once he grumbled, "For lodging nine months in your womb, I have had to pay a very high price."

A hero must fight, and know all the skills of warfare and self-defence.

For Alexander, to be at war was to be in a state of grace. War was a way of life: "What nobler way to die, than in battle? What greater gift can you offer the gods than your life? Is it not a sure way to paradise? I tell you the gods care not that you fight, but how you fight."

A hero needs a horse.

What kind of horse would our hero get for himself? A horse like the one which pulls the chariot of the moon goddess, Selene, with noble head, fanning tail and flaring nostrils? A horse like Pegasus — a mighty godlike horse, a dancing horse, a wild and untamed horse? Or a powerful war horse, many hands high, with sinews of iron and muscles like rope, that could carry the weight of armour?

This is how Alexander got his horse.

One day a stallion was brought to King Philip, but when he went to view it, a scene of commotion met his eyes. It was a young, unbroken, black war horse, leaping and bucking and rearing out of control. A poor groom was trying desperately to bring it to order, and others, too, ran out to try. But none could calm the animal, let alone mount it.

Philip was furious. He had paid a lot of money for the horse. "Send it back," he ordered.

Thirteen-year-old Alexander saw the fine head and powerful body, the flaring nostrils and pounding hooves, and he protested. "It's a pity to send away such a fine horse, just because there's no one with enough courage or skill to control it."

Philip was scornful of his boastful young son. "You have the impudence to criticize your elders. Are you telling me you could do any better?"

"Certainly," answered Alexander. "Let me show you."

"How will you pay for your rashness if you fail?" asked Philip.

"I'll pay for the horse," declared Alexander.

Then he took the leading rein, ducking the flying hooves and thrusting head, and pulled the horse round to face the other way. Murmuring soft words, he gradually quietened it enough to enable him to leap onto its bare back. The horse reared, bucked and twisted, doing everything it could to shake him off, but Alexander, with his thighs gripped tight, held his seat, loosening and tightening the rein by turns, and speaking to the animal with quiet words. At last the horse gave in and allowed Alexander to coax him into a trot, and then into a canter. Soon he was galloping round triumphantly in complete control.

The grooms and onlookers were astounded. How had this mere boy done what they had failed to do?

"Easy," answered Alexander. "I realized that the horse was afraid of its own shadow, so I turned him round into the sun."

"Seems to me that you must find a bigger world to inhabit," murmured his father wonderingly. "Macedonia will be too small to contain you."

The horse became Alexander's. He called it Bucephalus which means ox, because the only bit of its body which wasn't shining black was a white mark like an ox's head on its forehead. The horse stayed with him for nearly twenty years, and carried him through his most famous battles. Bucephalus never let anyone other than Alexander ride him and, after he died in India, Alexander named a city after him: Bucephala.

A hero must prove himself in battle.

Ah, Alexander! Just a young child, but so impatient to learn how to lead and how to fight battles. Whenever generals came to the palace, he was always tagging along listening to their exploits, asking questions about their campaigns and conquests. He excelled at chess and was brilliant at tactics and strategies.

Everyone was amazed that this young boy understood so much about warfare. He was already so brave, audacious and wise and capable of understanding the affairs of state that, by the time he was a teenager, his father, King Philip, sent him as an envoy to parts of his empire. On one occasion, Philip even left him in charge of the kingdom while he was away on a campaign.

But Alexander wanted more. He wanted to fight; to experience the heat of battle. How else could he become a hero?

So his father allowed him to lead his own campaign. An uprising broke out among the tribes of Thrace, and Alexander, aged only sixteen, was sent with a contingent of cavalry to put them down.

Leading from the front, he took his troops into the fray, charging into battle on Bucephalus, not for vain glory, but to show he valued his life no more than that of the lowest of his soldiers. He never expected his men to do anything he himself wasn't prepared to do. And so they loved him as a brother, and were prepared to follow him to the ends of the earth. With bravery, intelligence and quick-witted strategies, Alexander proved his military genius was equal to his father's. He routed the enemy and, as if to proclaim it to the world, founded the first city to bear his name: Alexandropolis.

The legend had begun.

Wreathed is the bull; the end is near, the sacrificer is at hand.

THE ILIAD

There was conspiracy in the air; intrigue, rage, assassination. Alexander's father, King Philip of Macedonia, leader of the Greeks, already had seven wives, and the politics and intrigue surrounding them were to bring him down. Marriage for the sake of maintaining power over conquered states was one thing, but to marry for love was quite another.

THE DEATH OF PHILIP

Philip fell in love with a princess called Eurydice. Alexander's mother, Olympias, was overcome with jealousy, and fury too, as any future son would be a threat to Alexander's succession. There were heated rows, and

Alexander even drew his sword on Philip, for which he and his mother were banished for a while.

What relief then, when Eurydice gave birth to a daughter. But later, just before Philip was due to set off on another campaign, she had a second child – and this time, it was a boy.

What would this mean to Alexander? Would his father prefer the new boy – born out of love – to him? Might Alexander no longer be favoured as his father's heir? The ambitious Olympias grappled with her jealousy. And then came another blow. Philip arranged for their daughter, Cleopatra, to be married to Olympias' brother, the King of Epirus. This would further alter the balance of power away from her, and possibly Alexander too.

Philip wanted this to be the most lavish wedding ever; one that would make a statement about his wealth and power and his godlike status. Hundreds of guests from all over the empire were invited to his palace at Aigai. They came by horseback, carriage and sea to find elaborate arrangements had been made in the Greek style, with banquets, athletics, drama, music and recitations. The culmination was to be a grand procession.

The sky was still black and glistening with stars when the guests, who had been asked to be seated by dawn, made their way to the outdoor theatre.

Everything was ready. The finest craftsmen had worked on huge images of twelve Greek gods, which included an image of Philip himself, which were to be paraded round the arena.

The sun was now up, the sky blue, the procession about to begin.

Philip approached the entrance to the arena flanked on either side by Alexander and his son-in-law, the King of Epirus. Suddenly, a young bodyguard named Pausanias secretly drew from its sheath a Celtic dagger, sharp, silver and double-edged, with dragons ornamenting the hilt, and, as Philip passed by, he leaped forward and plunged it deep between his ribs.

Philip lay dying. In the horror and confusion, Pausanias escaped. Three noblemen set off in hot pursuit. It seemed the assassination had been planned, for there were horses and helpers waiting for him at the town gates. But just as Pausanias came in sight of them, he caught his foot in a vine, tripped and fell. His pursuers were on him like a pack of hounds.

It isn't known if Pausanias was mercifully killed on the spot, or whether he was taken back to the city to be executed in the Greek way – clamped to a wooden board and left to starve to death in public.

Who was behind the crime? Who was the instigator of this murder? Was it Olympias, Alexander's mother, always scheming and interfering? Was it Alexander, afraid his inheritance would be taken from him by his new half-brother? Was it an order from Athens, where the Greeks still burned with indignation, having been beaten at the battle of Chaeronea by Philip? Did the Athenians and the Persians collude, both having reason to fear the Macedonian Philip? Or was it paid for by Persian gold given by Darius to Demosthenes, the democratic leader of Athens, who loathed being under the yoke of a Macedonian?

Rumours abounded, but whatever the truth, Alexander was instantly pronounced King of Macedonia and all the Greek territories.

CHAPTER TWO

ALEXANDER, THE EMPEROR

The year is 336 BC and Alexander is only twenty years old. And yes, he has become ruler over the Greek empire, and inherited everything from the Danube and the Dalmatian coast, to Greece and the islands of the Aegean. Following in the footsteps of such a powerful father as Philip, can he establish his leadership and authority? Can he reinforce his control over the Greek city states who, all too often, break up into factions and fight among themselves? True, his military expertise is famous, as are his powers of diplomacy, but don't forget, Alexander is a Macedonian, not a Greek. Has he the ability and skills to retain the loyalty of all his subjects: the Thracians, Illyrians, Paeonians and Thessalians ... and above all, the proud Athenians?

As soon as it was heard that Philip was dead, there were uprisings across the empire from Thrace to Greece. Alexander had powerful enemies in Athens, not least Demosthenes. The Greeks were trying to re-establish their rule. He had to act swiftly. It was no good simply quelling an uprising

by force; that way empires were quickly won but just as quickly lost, so he combined brutal force with democratic participation in an effort to bring stability back to the empire his father had created. When he heard that there were uprisings among the Balkan tribes far away to the north, he took an army all the way to the Danube to establish his northern borders, quelling Thracians and Triballians among the thick hostile forests and rivers.

Many of these fighters belonged to tribes from beyond the Balkans, whose origins are mysterious: the Scythians, who had roamed the steppes of Siberia, and had spread across the pasture lands of Europe and Central Asia; and the descendants from the tribes of Hunor and Magyar, who spread down to the plains of Hungary from the Carpathian mountains of Romania, to the banks of the Danube and the coasts of Dalmatia. The Scythians were famed and dreaded as the most amazing horse-riding archers, later fighting with both Alexander and Darius of Persia. All these tribes carried their own extraordinary stories – told again and again – about dense forests and mountains, lakes and pastures, reminding them of home.

Gathered round their flickering campfires at night, shivering at the sound of the wolf packs howling in the forests, Alexander's men listened in awe.

Pull your fur cloaks tighter round your bodies; come closer, and hear about the story of The White Stag.

T H E   W H I T E   S T A G

Somewhere among the Carpathian hills of eastern Europe, as the great red sun was setting in a blank waterless sky, Nimrod, the old leader of the tribe, stood alone and mourned. His sorrow was born out of the despair he felt for the survival of his people. A terrible scourge had struck their lands; it had dried up the soil so that nothing grew, it had drained the rivers and streams, so there were no fish, and there were no more animals to hunt in the shrivelled forests.

Nimrod had been having dreams and visions. They spoke to him of a Promised Land, but never told him where this land might be. Could it be far and beyond the snow-capped mountains which gleamed over in the west?

He gazed pityingly upon his two noble sons, Hunor and Magyar. With their intelligence, warrior skills and horsemanship, they were the best of all the tribe, and no one, no one, could read the signs of the sun, moon, fire and water as they could. But at that moment, all his dreams of passing on his leadership to them seemed as arid as the land. Was it all to be wasted?

His people lay listlessly around their fire waiting to suck at some roots and leaves simmering in the pot. Only Hunor and Magyar paced up and down, urgently discussing their plan to set off and look for some other place where they could find food. But which direction should they take?

Someone gasped, "Look!"

All eyes turned in the direction of the pointing finger. There, outlined against the setting sun, stood a giant stag — bigger than any they had ever seen. His body gleamed as white as the snow, and the sun, streaming through his antlers, seemed to turn them to gold.

Men leapt to their feet, grabbing their bows. This was the first animal they had seen for days and days, and they longed to catch it, so that, at last, they could all eat again. But Hunor and Magyar were the quickest. They jumped onto their horses and, as the White Stag leapt away, they set off in hot pursuit.

How hard they rode, all through the night, on and on through valley and forest, but every time they caught him in their sights and fitted an arrow, the stag sprang away like some enchanted spirit. Sometimes, he seemed close enough to touch, yet still they couldn't catch him. But they didn't give up. "Follow him!" whispered Magyar, and all the branches seemed to sway and murmur, "Follow him," and the streams and the wind seemed to echo his words, "Follow him!"

So they followed him across plains and rivers, up into mountains and down into deep valleys. It was dawn when, with their horses stumbling with exhaustion, they reached the edge of a blue lake, coiling with mist.

"Look, brother, look!" exclaimed Hunor.

The White Stag was there, at the water's edge, drinking deeply.

Silently they fitted arrows to their bows, but were too awestruck to let them fly.

The White Stag raised its head, pawed the shore three times, shook its antlers, and stepped into the white mist enveloping the lake. By the time Hunor and Magyar had come to their senses, the White Stag had disappeared.

Cursing their hesitation, they scoured the edge of the lake, looking for any trace of the stag so that they could resume the hunt, but as they searched, they became aware that the lake was full of fish, flowers perfumed the air and all the trees around were laden with fruit.

With great joy, the brothers realized that they had found a rich and luscious land which could save their starving people.

They immediately wheeled round their horses and set off for home, but, strange to say, though the White Stag had led them to the land of plenty in just one night, it took the two brothers seven moons to return to their tribe.

Just when Nimrod and his people had despaired of ever seeing Hunor and Magyar again, two riders appeared on the horizon: the sons of Nimrod! Their saddlebags were bulging with provisions and slung with game. Excitedly, they told how they had found a land of plenty – a paradise – which could sustain them all.

Old Nimrod embraced his sons with gratitude. They had fulfilled his visions and found the Promised Land. But he knew that his eyes were dimming, and that by the next sunset he would be dead.

He spoke to his people. "You have seen the sun setting on a day that will be remembered forever – even after we are all nothing but dust. Before this day is out and my life is done, pledge allegiance to my sons, Hunor and Magyar, respect and obey them, and let them lead you to this Promised Land." Then, like a giant tree which had been felled, Nimrod crashed to the ground.

With sadness, they built a huge mound over his body, and the next day they gathered together all their belongings. In a long line, the people followed their new leaders, Hunor and Magyar, along the trail of the White Stag, until they reached the blue lake and the Land of Plenty. Here they settled, and prospered greatly.

After quelling these northern tribes, and incorporating their warriors into his army, Alexander swiftly turned back again to Greece, hearing that the troublesome city of Thebes was in revolt.

THEBES

Thebes, the birthplace of Heracles, with a bloody warlike history, had always been a thorn in King Philip's side, ever since he had conquered it in the Battle of Chaeronea in 338 BC. Taking advantage of Philip's death, Thebes was trying to throw off Macedonian rule, perhaps thinking they could ignore such a young emperor as Alexander.

In an incredible fourteen days, Alexander marched his troops from Illyria to Thebes. At first he tried all he could to reason and bargain with the Thebans and even offered them a pardon, but when they stubbornly refused to surrender, Alexander mobilized his army with devastating results. Surrounding the city, he burst through and slaughtered more than 6,000 Thebans, the loss to Alexander being only 500 men. 30,000 were taken into slavery. As further punishment for Theban intransigence, he then allowed his Thracian soldiers to raze the city to the ground, killing, raping and pillaging at will. It was a shocking assault, which terrified his enemies. But Alexander knew the power of fear and, in the city of Thebes, he demonstrated extreme harshness with his enemies. This must be an example to all Greece.

And then came the Lady of Timoclea.

She was a noble Theban lady from the House of Timoclea, who had a reputation for high moral virtue. When she was attacked and raped by Thracian tribesmen fighting with Alexander, there was outrage. The leader of the tribesmen demanded that she show him where she had hidden the family wealth. She took him to a well, and when he bent over to look, she pushed him in and stoned him to death before being dragged away by the soldiers.

THE LADY OF
TIMOCLEA

Bound in chains, the Thracians led her and her children before Alexander. Expecting that she would receive severe punishment, she stood before him, proud and upright.

Alexander asked, "Who are you?"

She replied, "I am the sister of Theogenes, a commander-in-chief who fought against your father, King Philip, for the freedom of Greece, and who died on the field of battle at Chaeronea."

Admiring her quiet dignity and courage, Alexander ordered that she and her children be set free.

CHAPTER THREE

THE CONQUEST BEGINS

334 BC. The horizon glows from end to end; wild animals wonder if it is the dawn. But it is the glow from thousands of fires; funeral fires, campfires and blazing torches which light up campsites and tents. They will burn night and day. In time, the glow moves on, as it has moved all the way from Macedonia. Men, women, children, eunuchs and concubines, servants and slaves, historians, poets, actors, musicians, philosophers, engineers, seers, astrologers and storytellers are on the move.

They follow an army. It is the army of King Alexander.

The army consisted of his own personal aristocratic Companion Cavalry, an elite made up of 1,500 men — many of them his old trusted school friends: his foster brother Cleitus, known as "Black" Cleitus; Philotas, son of his father's general, Parmenion, who also rode with Alexander: Ptolemy and Callisthenes, the historian who had been taught by Aristotle; and his own personal prophet and seer, Aristander, who he consulted day by day. But especially, there was his best friend, the love of his life, Hephaistion, who was never far from his side. Like Achilles, who had loved Patroclus, Alexander loved Hephaistion. The noble Hephaistion had been the greatest love of his life right from school days, and was at his side until death parted them. Their helmets and breastplates gleamed, and their flowing red cloaks billowed as they rode. The Companion Cavalry didn't carry shields, as their strength was in moving lightly and swiftly, but wielded short dogwood spears for stabbing enemy horsemen. Their shields were carried by the Companion foot soldiers.

The iron in the soul of the army was the infantry, made up of 40,000 Macedonian peasants. Each foot soldier carried a sarissa — a long eighteen-foot spear made of cornel wood and tipped with metal — and when they were all clustered together on the field of battle, they moved in the wedge and phalanx formations as devised by Philip, and were virtually impenetrable. Also, drawn from all over the Greek territories, were Thracians, Odrysians, Triballians, Illyrians, Paeonians and Athenians. They were foot soldiers, javelin throwers, archers, slingers and horse warriors.

By day, Alexander's army travelled from one battle scene to the next. By night, they lit the funeral pyres for the dead, and celebrated victories with dance, music, poetry and games. As they met new peoples, religions and alien tribes, they asked, "What gods do you worship? How powerful are your demons and fairies?" The stories flowed like streams. The storytellers told old stories and learned new ones. They re-wove them to take in new events, and embroidered new events with old legends.

Every evening, after a day's battle, or the hard work of foraging for food in alien countries, they gathered round the campfires and listened to stories.

Every evening, Alexander and his generals consulted the seers, and asked

Aristander to interpret the omens. What was the meaning of the swallow which fluttered round Alexander's head, or the eagle which perched on the yoke of a plough, or the thunder and lightning in the night?

They struggled down the precipitous icy mountains of Macedonia and Thrace. Savage tribes lurked, ready to attack. When these wild people rolled wagons down the mountainside to crush the Macedonians, Alexander made his men lock shields in formation and lie down on the ground with their shields on top of them so that when the wagons rolled over them they were saved from being crushed.

They tramped through the tangled forests as dark as night, menaced by lions and wild boar. Horses and men stumbled down the steep canyons into deep rocky gorges and rushing rivers, quelling many uprisings on the way.

Riding ahead was Alexander on his trusty war horse, Bucephalus. He never hid from his enemies, never lurked at the back in safety, but was always defiantly visible and identifiable by his helmet, with its distinctive, white, fluttering egret feathers.

"Macedonia is too small for you," Alexander's father Philip had once commented. Alexander probably thought so too – and not just Macedonia, but all his territories, including Greece.

Now that his father's empire was back in firm hands, Alexander turned his attention to a larger empire in Asia. What greater challenge could there be than to engage with the old enemy of the Greeks – the Persians?

There were ancient scores to settle. Greece and Persia had been rivals and enemies for hundreds of years. Alexander's aim was to reclaim territory which had once been Greek, and overthrow the Persian Empire.

Now ruled by Darius III, the Persian Empire was the greatest power on earth. They had conquered all the land from west to east from Egypt to the River Indus, and north to south from the Jaxartes River to the Persian Gulf. The mighty Royal Road, the Achaemenid Highway, ran all the way from Mesopotamia to the Upper Euphrates, Babylonia and Susa. Other highways and routes linked it to Egypt and even to as far away as India. All were travelled by Darius' armies, and protected by his sentinels. They ruled much of Asia Minor, land which had been part of the Greek Empire, and once the Persians had even got as far as Athens. Ah, Alexander! The humiliation still burned in the inherited memory.

So he began to plan his campaign, beginning with Troy. Troy; the Troy of Homer and Helen of Troy, which Achilles and the Greeks had fought for and won in 1200 BC, was in the hands of the Persians.

Troy was the symbol; Troy was embedded in the Greek mind; it was a land where heroes – Greek and Trojan – had fought and died. It was the city sung about by Homer in the *Odyssey* and the *Iliad* and in the stories of Aeneas and the Wooden Horse. The city for ever linked with Helen, wife of Menelaus, with Hector, Prince of Troy and, most importantly, with Alexander's idol, Achilles.

The army advanced down to the coastal plains of Thrace. There before them was the ocean and the glittering waters of the Hellespont, all that divided them from Asia and the ancient city of Troy.

The next day, Alexander would see Troy for the first time.

THE STORY OF ACHILLES

It was prophesied that Achilles, son of the goddess Thetis and a mortal, the great warrior Peleus, would be an even greater warrior than his father, but that he was doomed to die in battle.

Thetis loved her son so dearly, she couldn't bear to think of the prophecy. Risking her own life, she carried him to the banks of the River Styx, the river which divides the living from the dead. Anyone who was submerged in these waters would live for ever. Holding her infant by one heel, she dipped his body into the waters and rejoiced.

She thought he was safe. But he wasn't. With what lamentation did Thetis learn that it had all been for nothing, and that Achilles was fated to die beneath the walls of Troy after he had killed his enemy, Prince Hector.

How could this be? Thetis realized it was because, when she had submerged her baby son in the waters of the Styx, she had held him by his heel. It was the only part of him that did not get wet, the only part of him that was unprotected. Achilles' heel would be his fatal weakness.

Thetis vowed that she would not leave her son to his fate. She sent him to the great Educator, the Centaur Chiron – half man, half horse – who had taught the finest warriors and heroes. Chiron taught Achilles all the arts of war, as well as wrestling, music, poetry and song – and by the time his studies were finished, Achilles was everything a Greek hero should be.

Alas, the day came which Thetis had dreaded. War broke out between Greece and Troy, because the Trojan prince, Paris, had stolen away the beautiful Helen, wife of King Agamemnon's brother, Menelaus. Achilles was called upon to join Agamemnon's fleet which was about to set sail and fight the Trojans for the return of Helen.

Thetis was grief-stricken. Her son was still so young. She did everything in her power to prevent Achilles joining the Greek fleet. She even disguised him as a girl and sent him away to the court of Lycomedes.

On the eve of going to war, the Greeks consulted the Oracle to find out whether their expedition was destined to succeed. The Oracle replied that it couldn't succeed without Achilles. But where was he? Messenger after messenger was sent, but no one could find him. At last, King Agamemnon ordered the mighty Odysseus to search for him.

Odysseus suspected that Achilles was in the court of Lycomedes, so he disguised himself as a pedlar and went there with a basket of enticing wares to sell to the ladies of the court. One by one, they came out and chose necklaces and bracelets, amulets and rings. But among all the trinkets, Odysseus had also placed a dagger. One closely veiled lady took up the weapon, and handled it with such skill, that Odysseus knew he had found Achilles.

Odysseus told Achilles how much they needed him. He begged him to fight with them against Troy, and very soon, Achilles, who was such a warrior at heart, and yearned for the excitement of battle, agreed to accompany Odysseus back to the fleet at Aulis.

CHAPTER FOUR

TROY

This Troy which Achilles and the Greeks had conquered a thousand years ago, was now in Persian hands. Alexander was determined to get it back. Not just to reclaim a symbol – Alexander's ambition went beyond symbols. With Troy conquered, the rest of the continent of Asia would spread before him all the way to India where, Aristotle had told him, he would reach the edge of the world.

Breathless with ambition and awe, Alexander and his men stared across the waters of the Hellespont separating Europe from Asia. This was the same strip of water which Achilles too had crossed on his way to fight the Trojan War.

CROSSING THE
HELLESPONT

It is the spring of 334 BC. Sixty ships wait to escort Alexander across the Hellespont. He himself takes the helm of the royal trireme, just as King Agamemnon had done in 1200 BC. Never forgetting his religious duties, Alexander prays each day. He knows the importance of keeping the gods on his side. In mid-crossing, he

orders a bull to be slaughtered and, like the ancient Greeks, sacrifices to the god of the ocean, Poseidon, by taking up the Cup of Heroes, and pouring sacred liquid into the waves to placate the Nereids — the sea nymphs. Voices, bells, reed pipes and piercing trumpets mingle with the slap of waves against the ship and the screech of gulls accompanies them on their way.

The coast of Asia drew closer. Before them was the Harbour of the Achaeans — named after the Greeks who landed there to fight the Trojan War. Alexander's eyes burned as he imagined the Achaean warriors preparing to leap ashore to fight the Trojans. Beyond the sand dunes and low hillocks, lay a flat, bleak plain stretching to where ancient Troy had stood as a vast city fort extending over hundreds of acres, with palaces, temples, towers, walls and citadels.

Alexander put on his suit of armour and took up his spear. He must be the first to touch Asian soil. As the boat came nearer to land, Alexander hurled his spear onto the shore. This was the first blow against the Persian Empire. Now the war had truly begun.

The Persians had a massive fleet of ships, yet not one of them was there to stop Alexander. Perhaps they thought he was too young, too weak, too poor to pose any threat. It was generations since the Greeks had won a battle against the Persians. Perhaps King Darius thought he was just an upstart, who could be swatted away at will, like a troublesome fly. But in Alexander's mind this was not just a war about empire. This was about destiny. He was a young man convinced that his destiny was to be a hero who would be remembered alongside all other heroes, and when the stories about him came to be written, they would speak of Alexander in the same breath as Hector, Rostam, Gilgamesh, Krishna and Achilles — especially Achilles.

The legendary city of Troy which Homer wrote about had long since been laid waste by wars and earthquakes. All that remained was a small village among the ruins of walls, palaces and ancient tombs spread over a vast area. Alexander's first act on reaching Troy was to search out the tomb of Achilles, so that he could honour his hero, while his best friend, Hephaistion, paid homage to Patroclus.

That night in Troy, lying in his tent, Alexander reached for his beloved copy of Homer's *Iliad*, and read about the dreadful but glorious battles between the Greeks and the Trojans.

ACHILLES' DESTINY

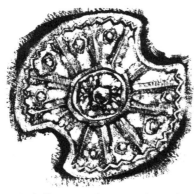

Hear how Helen, the beautiful wife of Menelaus of Greece, had been stolen away by Paris, Prince of Troy.

Agamemnon had rallied together a fleet of a thousand ships and the finest warriors to go and fight the Trojans and bring back Helen. Among them was Achilles, the greatest champion among the Achaeans.

Achilles was keen and ready to go to war, but his mother, Thetis, did everything she could to prevent her son leaving. "Your life will be brief. If only you could be free of cares and sorrows now, for you will not last long, o child of mine, short-lived among men, and to be so pitied."

But Achilles knew it was his destiny.

There was only one other warrior who could be compared to Achilles,

and that was his enemy, the noble Hector, son of King Priam of Troy and Queen Hecuba.

The bards sang of Troy, and of the bravery and courage of both sides. Fortunes swung with the whim of the gods, first this way, then that, without any clear notion as to who would win. Then Achilles had a quarrel with his own king, Agamemnon, and was so furious with him that he withdrew to his tent and refused to fight. From that moment, the Greeks began to get the worst of it, and it seemed the Trojans were winning.

The Greeks were in despair and felt abandoned by the gods. If only Achilles would come out and fight. At last, Achilles' dearest and most beloved friend, Patroclus, went to him in his tent and begged him to come to the rescue; so many of his comrades had died. But still Achilles was sulky and adamant. Then Patroclus remembered how even the sight of Achilles' armour brought terror to the enemy and made them flee, so he asked Achilles if he might wear his armour and carry his shield.

> *"Give the Greeks some gleam of hope.*
> *Give me the armour from thy shoulders.*
> *Give me thy mail to wear,*
> *So that the Trojans, at the sight of me,*
> *May think I am Achilles, and may pause*
> *From fighting. Then the warlike sons of Greece,*
> *Tired as they are, may breathe once more, and gain*
> *A respite from the conflict."*

So Achilles gave Patroclus his glittering mail. Patroclus put it on and led the Greek warriors into battle.

Everyone knew Achilles' armour. How often it had struck dread into the heart of his enemies. Achilles was so savage and merciless in war, that even his friends were horrified. At the sight of his fearsome armour, the Trojan soldiers wavered. Achilles was back, they thought, and they feared for their lives.

But suddenly, Hector appeared; glorious heroic Hector, Hector the Horse Tamer. Patroclus found himself face to face with this mighty Trojan hero. He was like a boar facing a lion. Hector raised his spear, aimed, and struck the death blow. Patroclus crashed to the ground, dead.

The Trojans cheered. "Hector has killed Achilles! The war must be over. The Trojans must be the victors." But when Hector stripped away the armour, he saw not Achilles, but Patroclus.

When Achilles heard of the death of his best friend, he was distraught with guilt and fury. He raged and wept, and descended into such dark despair that everyone feared for him. His mother, Thetis, goddess of the ocean, arose from her cave beneath the sea and came to comfort him. But Achilles told her, "I must avenge my friend's death and kill Hector," even though he knew that it was prophesied that he himself would die soon after Hector.

Desperate to keep her son alive as long as possible, Thetis entreated him to wait a day while she obtained a new suit of armour for him, and she sped away to the god Hephaestus – the Divine Armourer.

While he waited, Achilles leaped upon the city wall and bellowed a dreadful heart-rending cry, which utterly terrified the Trojans.

Meanwhile, silver-footed Thetis arrived in the radiant, bronze-constructed, imperishable and starry dwelling of Hephaestus, and set him to work straight away to make her son a suit with armour of divine qualities.

Thetis returned the next day bringing marvellous weapons, and a suit of armour which only a god could have forged. Achilles put it on, and sprang into his chariot, yelling hoarse war cries. With deadly sorrow and hatred burning in his eyes, he went in search of Hector.

At first Hector fled, but Achilles taunted him for his cowardice. At last Hector stopped. He turned and faced Achilles, suddenly brimming with reckless courage. The two warriors fell upon each other with thundering blows. Their struggles churned up the dust, so that the two men disappeared, and all that could be heard was the clash and thud of blows, and metal against metal.

At last action ceased. There was a terrible silence. Who was the victor? As the dust settled, the watchers saw Achilles binding Hector's body to his chariot.

Maddened by grief, Achilles was pitiless in victory. Nine times, he galloped round the city, dragging the corpse behind him, before the very eyes of Hector's horrified parents. Finally, he abandoned it near the funeral pyre of his beloved friend, Patroclus. Grief-stricken, Hector's father came to Achilles to plead for the return of his son's body. Achilles was moved by the old king's dignity in sorrow, and finally allowed the hero's body to be removed for proper death rites.

With Hector dead, Achilles knew that he too was doomed to die and

that the Fates had almost finished spinning the thread of his own life. He plunged back into battle, leading his men towards the gates of the city, known as the Scaean Gates. There he was glimpsed by Paris of Troy, Paris who had caused the war by stealing Helen, and who was still unwilling to return her to her husband, Menelaus. Paris now took up his bow and aimed at Achilles. He let fly his arrow. O fatal arrow, how surely did it speed on its deadly path; not to strike Achilles' god-given armour, nor his shield of bronze, but the one part of him uncovered by his sandal.

Achilles' heel was pierced; the heel his mother had held when she dipped him into the sacred life-giving waters of the Styx; the heel which was unprotected; his weakest spot.

And so the prophecy came true. Achilles died beneath the walls of Troy, and his ashes were placed in the same urn as those of Patroclus.

For Alexander the story was as fresh as if it had happened yesterday. Inspired, he went to the temple in Troy, and took possession of a suit of armour which was known to be Achilles', and also took down Achilles' shield, which had been hanging there since the Trojan War. From then on, this armour travelled with him everywhere — even as far as India. It was an inspiration, and sometimes he wore it to give him courage, reminding him of those ancient heroes.

O heroes! Remember that battles don't just bring glory, but also heart-rending sorrow which comes with the deaths of comrades.

CHAPTER FIVE

PERSIA: ON ENEMY SOIL

Alexander was now on Persian territory, which had once belonged to Greece.

The Persians worshipped a god called Ahura Mazda. He was the god of the sky, sometimes appearing like a sun with wings, at other times as a bearded figure, accompanied by winged lions, scorpion men and bulls with men's heads. The Persian emperor, Darius III was worshipped as Ahura Mazda, their supreme god on earth.

Over generations, Persian rule had been unassailable, their wealth unimaginable, their resources seemingly endless. The Persians had beaten the Greeks many times. What did it matter if Alexander had crossed the Hellespont with his army? Darius didn't stop him. Perhaps he would send a modest army to deal with Alexander in his own good time.

With very little challenge, Alexander continued his campaign through Lydia, along the rocky Aegean coast, conquering the small coastal towns with ease, riding up and down beside his troops, the white plumes of egret's feathers fluttering on his helmet.

But where were the Persians?

One day in mid-May, a small cloud of dust heralded the return of a scouting party. They came galloping into camp with news! A Persian army had secretly been massing and was waiting for them on the other side of the River Granicus.

A shiver of excitement ran through the men. This was the moment Alexander had been waiting for; the moment when he would meet his mighty, ancient enemy face to face. At last, he could prove to the world and himself that neither the Persians nor death held any fears for him.

It is still spring in the year 334 BC.

THE BATTLE OF
GRANICUS

Thousands of camp followers have settled themselves down, preparing for the battle to come: putting up shelter, foraging for food, filling water pitchers, lighting fires and cooking meals. The air is resounding with voices, music and war dances.

On the western banks of the River Granicus, Alexander's troops had pitched their tents; they concentrated on sharpening their weapons, grooming their horses and checking their body armour. On the east side of the river, the Persians were doing the same.

The two armies of the Greeks and the Persians faced each other across the swift flowing waters. Both saw problems, and decisions needed to be made. Each weighed up the odds and consulted the oracles.

For the Greeks, the first problem was that Alexander, "Ruler of the Greek Empire including Athens", was a Macedonian and not a Greek. This angered and alienated many Greeks, and thousands of them had already joined up with the Persians to fight against him as mercenaries.

For the Persians, on the other hand, the general of the Persian army was a Greek called Memnon, and when it came to fighting the Greeks, the Persians didn't always trust him.

King Darius hadn't taken Alexander seriously. After all, the eminent Athenian orator, Demosthenes, had dismissed him as a simple-minded boy and a buffoon. As far as Darius was concerned, he was a young upstart, with little experience, so he only sent 35,000 men to fight at Granicus, whereas Alexander had an army of about 50,000.

Darius' army was drawn from the colonies of the Persian Empire; Bactrians, Medes and Greeks, from the Caspian and Oxus to the mountains of Cappadocia. They wore very heavy metal armour, whereas Alexander's soldiers wore light body armour and carried light arms such as javelins and wooden lances. The Persians thought they would easily be defeated.

But Memnon had heard enough about Alexander to be wary. He advised his superiors to carry out a scorched earth policy first. "Alexander doesn't carry provisions but lives off the land," he said, "so burn the fields, and starve the Greeks into defeat."

But they didn't trust him, and Memnon was overruled, his Persian masters deciding to fight straight away.

Alexander too was keen to fight, but Parmenion and the other generals looked at the situation and were pessimistic. Even though they had more men, the Persians had the best position on the far side where the banks rose steeply, and the river ran deep and fast. They argued with Alexander.

"This could be a death trap. It's a dangerous place to cross."

"If I've crossed the Hellespont, I can cross the Granicus," retorted Alexander.

"Moreover, it's the month of Daisios," they reasoned, "and Macedonians never fight in that month."

"Well then, we'll change the calendar," said Alexander, and he changed it to the month of Artemisios.

"But look at the Persians," pleaded his generals, "they are heavily armoured. The horses and their riders have metal sheets to protect their legs and flanks; the horses wear headpieces and breastplates and their riders, metal-plated armour combined with a metal helmet. They will be protected from strikes and blows."

"All the better," said Alexander. "With all that weight, the Persians will move slowly and heavily, and be unable to manoeuvre quickly."

He was right. With their lighter helmets and breastplates, Alexander's men could move swiftly and were more agile with their javelins, and especially with their wooden thrusting lances – the sarissas – which Philip had taught Alexander to use with such devastating effect.

So Alexander brushed aside the worries of his generals. He was impatient, and wanted to attack immediately. But again his generals shook their heads reluctantly. "No, no. You can't fight straight away," they said. "The men need time to get into battle lines; they are tired from walking ten miles a day; it is late afternoon and nearly dark. The Persians never fight before sunrise."

"Good, then I'll attack before sunrise!" cried Alexander.

The Persians had camped where the river was deepest and most speedy,

and the banks were steep and muddy. They rested for the night, thinking this would be an easy victory. They assumed that Alexander, on the far bank, would attack from the front, and were sure that his men would flounder in the slithery, slippery conditions.

But Alexander was not just stubborn, he was cunning. He knew how to make the enemy think one thing, while he did another. As soon as the sun went down, he took a contingent of cavalry under cover of darkness, and crept silently along the riverbank until he found a safe crossing over to the eastern shore. They crossed the River Granicus and bivouacked quietly. Just before daylight, with terrifying war cries, Alexander and his men charged into battle, attacking where the enemy least expected it, from behind.

Too late, the slumbering Persians tried to cover their backs and still face the Greeks opposite on the western shore. But the Greek soldiers, with their long sarissas, formed a phalanx to cover their comrades crossing the river, while Alexander's cavalry came galloping in from behind.

There was confusion among the Persians. A fierce battle in the water ensued. The Persian soldiers slithered down the muddy banks and, weighed down by their heavy armour, floundered about, unable to crawl back.

Hundreds drowned in the river or were hacked to pieces. The rest retreated onto the eastern plain. With joy, Alexander went after them with his cavalry.

The Persians reformed and spread their cavalry out as widely as possible along a front line, while holding their infantry in reserve. Visible to everyone was Alexander in his magnificent armour, his blazoned shield and his distinctive helmet.

By now, all of Alexander's columns were across the river, and he deployed them into battle formation. Again, he used trickery. The Persians thought that he was preparing to attack them on the right wing, so they quickly transferred some of their best troops from the centre to deal with the threat. This was exactly what Alexander had predicted. He went into a classic "pivot attack". His left wing formed the axis as his men charged in a wedge formation. He pretended to head for the left wing instead of the right, but then suddenly swung his wedge into the weakened centre. Meanwhile, Parmenion fought off the contingents of Medes and Bactrians on the left flank.

There was a pitched battle.

The air rang with the clash and crash of metal on metal; horses heaved and reared, javelins flew, scimitars sliced, blood flowed.

Alexander's spear was broken on the first assault. Demaratus of Corinth tossed him his own. Now Alexander charged towards Mithridates, son-in-law of the Persian King. Mithridates hurled his spear at Alexander with such force that it pierced the shield and struck the cuirass behind. Alexander flung it aside and then thrust his spear deep into the Persian prince's breastplate. The breastplate held, but Alexander's spear snapped in two. Mithridates went for his sword, but Alexander hurled his broken spear into his opponent's face. He didn't see another enemy horseman pounding up behind him with a flying sabre. The horseman struck Alexander's helmet with such force that it penetrated his scalp through to the bone. Alexander swung round and killed him, but slid from his horse, swaying and stumbling about with dizziness.

Out of the dust swirled another Persian. He galloped up with swinging

sword and was about to deal Alexander the death blow, but Alexander's friend and foster brother, "Black" Cleitus, saw what was about to happen, and struck first, severing the attacker's arm. Alexander managed to clamber back onto his horse, and the battle raged on.

The Greek phalanx was now pouring through the Persian centre and had begun to make short shrift of the infantry behind. The Persians abandoned their flanks for the centre, but were caving in all round and, as Parmenion demolished the left with his cavalry, Darius' army broke up and fled.

The Persians tried to reassemble on a high knoll. A herald was sent asking Alexander for a truce. But Alexander was in no mood to relax now. He was out to destroy them. His phalanx attacked the front. The deadly criss-cross of a thousand long sarissas caged and fenced them in, while the cavalry hemmed them in from the rear.

Those who could, turned and fled, the others died or were captured.

The night was filled with howling and wailing for the dead, as bodies were collected from the field of battle and the funeral pyres lit.

To the 1,500 mercenary Greeks fighting with the Persians, Alexander's men showed no mercy. All were put to death, but for 2,000 – the lowest ranked – who were bound in fetters and sent to Macedonia as slave labour. It was a lesson to all Greeks. You were either with Alexander or against him. This was the true nature of Alexander. He could not stand betrayal or treachery; he killed ruthlessly but not aimlessly. Like a true warrior, he upheld the code of conduct, and honoured his opponents. He allowed the Persians to gather up their dead so they could be given the proper rites, for Alexander was not just a military man but a king –

of education and ideals. It was never enough for him to win battles; he wanted to rule, and to do this he had to build up loyalty, even among those he had captured.

Alexander's own men were given honourable funerals, especially his dead Companions, whose funerals were glorious, and whose families were generously compensated. Although the triumph of Granicus was his, he wanted to show the Greeks back home that, though he was a Macedonian, he considered the Macedonians and Greeks as one against the Persians. He ordered all the Persian treasures that he had captured at Granicus to be sent to Athens for dedication at the temple to the goddess Athena and, with a magnificent stroke of diplomacy, labelled them with these words: "Alexander, son of Philip and the Greeks (excepting the Spartans) on behalf of the barbarians who live in Asia Minor."

He wanted to emphasize that he claimed the spoils of the enemy on behalf of all Greece, and not for his own personal gain.

CHAPTER SIX

"LORD OF ALL ASIA"

Throughout the summer of 334 BC, Alexander and his army continue along the coast of Asia Minor; freeing cities from Persian rule and setting up democracies in the Greek style. Some welcome him, some fight him. Hundreds of camp followers come in his wake.

They captured the fine harbour town of Ephesus, famous for trade, fishing and the wild boar that roamed the wooded hills behind. It had once been Greek, then Persian, then Greek, and was now Persian again. It was in Ephesus that the great temple to the Greek goddess, Artemis, had burned to the ground the night Alexander was born. Everyone had said at the time that it was an omen, and that one day Asia too would burn, but the Persians had built their own temple on top of the temple to Artemis, dedicating it to their goddess, Anahita.

EPHESUS

Anahita was the High, the Powerful, the Immaculate; born of water; Anahita was the purifier, who gave life by creating lakes and rivers and

milk; worshipped for her wisdom, she was like the Greek goddess, Aphrodite, also the goddess of love.

Alexander saw a wonderful effigy of Anahita as Queen on Earth. She wore a crown of stars with flashing beams of light; she was clothed in a gold brocade coat, with otter furs; she was festooned with jewels, dangling earrings, necklaces and girdles. He was impressed, but now that Ephesus was Greek once more, he wanted the temple restored to Artemis, and he himself honoured as the new god-emperor, the new Zeus.

To celebrate their victory, Alexander held games. There was feasting, with music and recitations. "A story, a story!" people begged the storytellers!

Draw near, then. See how the sparks of night fires spiral up to the stars. Remember the story of Artemis, the Huntress and Queen of the Night, and how she loved Orion!

ARTEMIS AND ORION

Orion was a skilled hunter. All day long, he hunted in the woods and forests, accompanied by his beloved dog, Sirius. He was fleet-footed as a deer, and his aim was true.

The goddess Artemis saw this marvellous hunter, who seemed almost as expert as she was. She fell in love with him. But her brother, Apollo, greatly disapproved of his sister loving a

mortal. He tried everything he could to cure her of her infatuation, but to no avail.

So one day, he cunningly tricked her into testing her skills as an archer by teasing and scorning her expertise as a markswoman. She protested and showed him over and over again how true her aim was. Then Apollo pointed far out to sea, where a distant speck rose and fell among the waves, and challenged his sister to strike it.

Artemis seized her bow and feathered an arrow. She fitted it to the string, aimed, and with mighty force let fly. She hit her target. The speck disappeared beneath the surface of the waves and did not re-emerge.

But Apollo had tricked her. She had killed her beloved Orion, who had been innocently swimming in the ocean. She wept bitter tears. And so that she would always be reminded of her beloved as she hunted through the night, Artemis turned Orion and his faithful dog Sirius into stars, and placed them as a glittering constellation in the sky.

Word spread quickly about Alexander's victory at Granicus, as his armies crossed the pine-terraced hills down to the coastal towns. Sardis, Ephesus and Priene had all fallen before his advance, some surrendering with barely a fight, preferring to return to life under the democracies of the Greeks, than continue beneath the repressive dictatorial regimes of the Persians.

The Persians began to take Alexander more seriously. He had reached the coastal town of Miletus. Darius sent war ships, hoping to lure him into battle at sea with the vast Persian fleet.

Although Alexander had mobilized his ships, and had won previous

battles at sea, he knew he couldn't match the superior numbers of the Persians, nor the supreme mastery of their Cypriot and Phoenician crews. However, when they were all gathered anxiously looking out to sea, his senior general, Parmenion, saw an eagle, the symbol of Zeus, sitting on the shore near one of Alexander's ships, surely a sign, he urged, that Alexander should take to sea and fight Darius' fleet. After all, the Greeks, too, were famed for their seamanship.

But to everyone's amazement, Alexander said he would disband his ships, pointing out that the eagle was sitting on land – "A sure sign that we can only win on dry land. We will beat the Persian fleet on land instead of at sea." And it was at the ports that he aimed his might.

It wasn't easy. Darius' ships harassed them in the harbour. Miletus was a heavily fortified stronghold with mighty walls and, during a fierce struggle, Alexander did indeed have to put his ships to sea, and, surprising the Persians with a sudden hostile attack, put their ships to flight.

At last, with Miletus taken, he moved on to Halicarnassus, where stood one of the seven wonders of the ancient world – the great Mausoleum. This city was an even mightier port with great fortifications. This was the point he had wanted Parmenion to understand; by capturing all the ports along the coast, he would defeat the Persian fleet.

The Siege of Halicarnassus

But Halicarnassus was not going to give in easily. The fight was long, bitter and messy. There were months of siege and deprivation. The soldiers got restless and drunk.

It nearly led to their downfall. But Alexander had patience, and though there were long periods of waiting and inaction, his brain was never still. He was always inventive, always thinking about what

to do, how to do it, when to do it; consulting his engineers and employing the latest techniques. Not for him the old traditional weapons, nor trying to win through sheer force of numbers. He ordered the building of siege engines, huge battering rams, giant catapults which could hurl burning torches. Then began the final assault. After a bloody battle when he nearly lost his life, Alexander and his men breached the walls of the castle and forts. Finally, Alexander could claim victory and move on along the coast; there were more towns and ports to capture.

Alexander headed along the Royal Road, the Achaemenid Highway, created by the earlier great Persian king, Darius I, urging his army onwards into the rugged highlands, winding up and down between rugged slopes and the coast, bringing town after town under his rule.

By the winter of 334 BC the southern regions of Asia Minor were under his control. A shivering chill descended, so Alexander decided to move his exhausted troops inland, and rest in the town of Gordium.

Gordium was the capital city of Phrygia, lying on the dusty ancient Royal Road which ran between Lydia and Assyria. It had seen better times when, several centuries earlier, Thracian tribes had settled there and created a large kingdom. Their kings had built over eighty great tombs with wooden chambers all covered over by artificial hills. Then one day, a tribe called the Cimmerians overran it and, after many fearsome battles, Gordium was laid waste.

At first, Alexander found it an unexciting place, situated among low, drab, barren hills — with nothing much to amuse the troops, nor to stir his curiosity. Then he learned that the local Phrygians had once come from his own country of Macedonia, and he heard of a local legend

which linked one of the largest hills in Gordium to the ancient Phrygian king, Gordius, and his son, Midas.

THE LEGEND OF GORDIUS

In ancient times lived a poor farmer called Gordius, who only had a small plot of land and two yokes of oxen to work it. One pair of oxen ploughed the land, while the other pulled his wagon.

One day, a strange thing happened. An eagle flew down and perched on the yoke of his plough. It stayed there all day until he had finished work and released the oxen. Feeling very troubled, Gordius set off for home, thinking he must consult a seer about this event. On his way he passed a well where a young woman was drawing water. He stopped for a drink and couldn't help telling the girl about the eagle. She said that as she came from a family of seers and soothsayers she was sure this was a miraculous sign, and that he should return immediately and make a sacrifice to the god, Zeus. The young woman went with him, and showed him how to perform the sacrifice. In due course Gordius married her, and they had a son called Midas – later of the Golden Touch.

Midas grew up to be a fine young man and he worked the same two pairs of oxen, one pair to till the land, the other to drive the wagon. Unrest broke out in the area. The Phrygians were fighting and at odds

with each other. Finally, they consulted the Oracle for help with their disputes. The Oracle told them that a wagon would come, bringing a king. At that moment, Midas drove up in the wagon bearing his ageing parents. The Phrygians were amazed. The Oracle had no sooner spoken, than the prophecy was fulfilled.

They made Midas King, and put him on the throne. His father, Gordius, was sure that this was the ultimate meaning of the eagle which had landed on his plough all those years ago and, to give thanks to Zeus, he and Midas took the wagon to the top of the acropolis. There they set the wagon and bound the yoke with cord made from the bark of a very hard fruit tree called the cornel tree. They bound it tight, in such a convoluted knot that no one could see where one end began and the other ended, and no one knew how to untie it.

For generations, this puzzle remained unsolved. Many people climbed the acropolis to marvel at the Gordian Knot. Some tried to undo it, for it was said, whoever loosed the knot would be the ruler of the Phrygians. But the knot remained tight and intractable as ever — and no one had managed to loosen it.

Spring was in the air. Alexander's reinforcement troops had arrived, and everyone prepared to leave Gordium.

But Alexander felt that he must first visit this wagon up on the hill, and see the knot for himself.

THE GORDIAN
KNOT

Unwilling to appear just another curious traveller, he pointed out that he was a Macedonian with a blood link to the Phrygians, and related to

Zeus. He claimed to have an ancestral and mythical link to the chariot. What better way to give him extra appeal and authority with these recently conquered subjects — especially after he had left — than to undo the knot.

So, with a band of men, Alexander climbed up to the acropolis where the chariot was kept. Everyone gathered round to watch. Alexander examined the knotted cord made of bark from the cornel tree, but couldn't find an end. He attempted to loosen in the knot with his fingers, but it remained stubbornly tight, and no matter how hard he tried, he couldn't undo the knot.

At last, fearing that he would lose face, Alexander took his sword and sliced through it. "I have done it!" he cried.

That night there was thunder and lightning which was joyfully interpreted as meaning that Zeus approved of the manner in which he had undone the Gordian knot. The natives accepted his action. It was admired as an example of his decisiveness, and from then on word spread far and wide, that Alexander had cut loose the Gordian Knot and that he was the rightful ruler of the Phrygians.

People were calling him "Lord of all Asia". But Alexander knew that, until he had defeated Darius, it was a false title.

There were months on the road, skirmishing and fighting various warlike tribes who roamed the region. Spring gave way to the searing heat of summer. It was July, 333 BC and day by day the temperatures rose relentlessly till it was burning hot; not a good time to fight any important battles. But news came that Alexander's old opponent, general Memnon, was dead and that, in Babylon, King Darius had amassed a

huge army for the battle of all battles, determined finally to lay low this impudent young man.

Alexander had no choice. He hurried south through the relentless heat from Ancyra into the arid, volcanic uplands of Cappadocia, desperately trying to reach the strategic coastal town of Tarsus on the other side before the Persians got to it.

By August they had ascended the great range of the Taurus Mountains. Up there, at nearly 4,000 metres, Alexander's men arrived at the pass known as the Cilician Gates, and were poised for a massive struggle with Darius' forces. This was the only route down to the plains of Cilicia. It was a deep twisting canyon – ideal for ambush – and, had they failed to push through, Alexander would have had to retreat.

However, Arsames, Persian governor of Cilicia, perhaps remembering Memnon's disregarded advice at Granicus, instead of defending the pass, had stayed down on the Cilician plains, destroying all the crops to deprive Alexander of food.

Alexander couldn't believe his luck. The small force at the Cilician Gates was soon annihilated. His entire army descended triumphantly, four abreast, to the plain and onwards to the city of Tarsus, the capital of Cilicia.

Alexander marched the army, driving it hard. News came that Arsames was attempting to sack the city and make off with its treasures. Parmenion rode on ahead with a contingent of men and put the citizens to flight, saving most of the wealth of the city, including its mint. Arsames, however, managed to escape and join Darius in Babylon.

Having endured a march through the blazing heat of the summer, it was

an utterly exhausted Alexander and his army who entered Tarsus on 3 September 333 BC.

They were weary, covered in dust and sweat. Running through Tarsus was the River Cydnus — flowing clear blue and chilled by the mountain snows. How could Alexander resist? He stripped off and plunged into the freezing waters.

It nearly killed him. The shock brought on cramps so severe that his men had to pull him out of the river, pale and half-drowned. He developed a raging fever and everyone was sure he would die.

Alexander's own personal physician, Philip of Acarnania, said he had a remedy — a fast-acting drug, but one whose side-effects could be drastic, if not fatal. Other physicians would have been afraid to act, fearing that if Alexander died, they would be blamed. Alexander, delirious and barely conscious, agreed to take the drug. At that moment a note arrived from Alexander's senior general, Parmenion. "Beware of the physician, Philip. I am informed that he has been bribed by Darius to kill you."

BEWARE THE
PHYSICIAN

With the note still in his hand, Alexander took up the goblet containing the medicine and, looking him in the eye, handed the note to Philip. As the physician read the note, Alexander drank the medicine.

Philip looked up in horror, but smilingly, Alexander handed back the empty goblet.

The effect of the potion was violent. Alexander lost his voice and was barely able to breathe. For three days and nights, Philip never left his side, but massaged him constantly and applied hot fermentations. The medicine was not poison and, slowly, Alexander pulled through. Though

weak and barely able to sit on his horse, he rode out to show himself to his troops as soon as he could, to prove that he was still alive. A great cheer resounded through the camp. Alexander prayed and made sacrifices to the gods, thanking them for his recovery.

But there was no time to slacken. A messenger brought disturbing news. Darius was on his way to Cilicia with a huge army, gathered together from all over his empire. Alexander calculated that Darius would command the pass at the Pillar of Jonah on the borders of Syria, and as he was still not fit enough for battle, he split his forces. He sent Parmenion with the cavalry eastwards along the coast to take the pass and report on the movements of the Persian king, while he rode westwards with the rest of the troops.

Alexander took his time, partly to allow himself to recuperate, but also because he never permitted himself to be rushed. He liked to bewilder the enemy – a tactic he was to use over and over again, going at his own pace rather than being forced by his enemy. It was September before he set off, meandering around here and there, fighting wild tribesmen, unsure of what was happening behind him, and where Darius was.

In October he received a message from Parmenion, that Darius had been spotted with a vast army, very close to the Pillar of Jonah and the Syrian border. Alexander immediately turned round and, by marching his men at the double, took the coast road, reaching the town of Issus in two days. While he waited for Parmenion to join him, he created a field hospital for those of his men who were either wounded or too exhausted by their forced march to carry on. As soon as Parmenion arrived, Alexander set off with a united army, back into the mountains, making for the pass at the Pillar of Jonah.

Meanwhile, Darius had entered Syria and chosen a plain on which to fight his battle. It was ideal; the ground was level, excellent for chariots, and a perfect space from which to command his huge army. It was also only two days' march to the mountain pass of the Syrian Gates. So, here the Persians waited for sight of the enemy.

The Persian king waited and waited, but Alexander didn't come. Darius hadn't heard of Alexander's illness and, when there was no sign of him, he began to think that Alexander had changed his mind about any further combat with the Great King. Besides, his spies and scouts reported back that Alexander was in Issus, reinforcing his communication lines and safeguarding his flanks.

So, amazingly, Darius somehow persuaded himself, or was persuaded by flattering courtiers, to leave the plain and go on the offensive, attacking Alexander where he thought he would find him — in Issus. His generals knew better and begged him not to risk losing his advantage, but Darius ignored them. He moved up into the narrow gorges and passes, through the Amanian Gates, the pass of Mount Amanus, and swooped down onto the town of Issus.

The same night that Darius entered Issus, expecting to find Alexander, Alexander reached the Pillar of Jonah, expecting to find Darius.

Unbeknownst to each other, the two armies had passed each other on either side of the Amanid mountains.

All Darius found in Issus was the field hospital Alexander had left for his wounded troops. Darius killed most of the wounded soldiers, while others had their limbs hacked off, leaving mutilated survivors to wander freely and instil fear, spreading the word that the Great King was on the warpath.

Alexander had now moved back to the coast and was in the town of Myriandrus, only fifteen miles away from Issus, when he heard the news that Darius had left his position on the wide Syrian plain and taken over the far narrower Issus Plain. He could hardly believe it. He knew that the Issus Plain was a difficult area, hemmed in between the coast, a river and the mountains. Had Darius really left his prime position?

Alexander sent a secret ship round the coast to see if it was true. Word came back, yes, and that the Bay of Issus was swarming with Persian warships.

Alexander was shocked. This would be a perilous battleground for both of them. There wasn't much room to manoeuvre. His generals thought the Persians had set a trap. Crossing a river with an army is always dangerous and here, there was nowhere to retreat to. They thought that Alexander had been wrong-footed, and that Darius had the upper hand.

CHAPTER SEVEN

THE BATTLE OF ISSUS

It is the last day of October in the year 333 BC.

Yesterday, when the men were gathered round their fires, they were nervous. Had Alexander over-reached himself? There were ripples of anxiety coming from the ranks. Could they really overcome the Great King? This was to be Alexander's first encounter with Darius himself.

But today, Alexander is calm, and seems unruffled by the news coming back to him – even though descriptions of the might and numbers of Darius' army should make the greatest warrior tremble.

Alexander could always turn bad news into good. He set about rallying his troops and boosting morale with a passionate speech to his men. "You are a victorious army fighting a vanquished one!" He told them that it was Darius who was trapped. Darius who, having left the broad plain in Syria, had hemmed in his armies on the narrow Issus Plain, between the Pinarus River and the mountains on one side, and the sea on the other – "Surely an intervention from the gods on our side," he declared.

He encouraged them to remember their strengths and what they would gain by their victory over the Medes and Persians. He spoke to them like a brother rather than a king, a fellow fighter, who would not hesitate to do whatever he asked them to do. "They only have Darius to lead them, you have Alexander!" he shouted.

As always, Alexander's enthusiasm and powers of persuasion worked, and the men felt reassured. Their energy surged back as they felt the thrill of battle in their veins.

Under the cover of darkness, Alexander turned his forces round, climbing through the night, back towards the Pillar of Jonah. Huddled and cold, among the rocks, the troops got what sleep they could, while Alexander made sacrifices to the gods of the sea and the night. The next day, they would descend down to the narrow plain between the river and the sea.

This is what happened on the first day of November, the day of the Battle of Issus.

At daybreak, fed and rested, the army rose in an orderly fashion. It was a twelve-mile march down to the battlefield, so, at first, Alexander kept his men in a single route column. As the ground opened up, he extended his line of troops, sending Parmenion across the River Pinarus to set up a left flank as far as the seashore. Alexander put himself and his cavalry squadrons to the right, as far as the foothills.

Now they were face to face with the enemy — and it was an awesome sight.

Spread before them, glittering through the smoke of thousands of campfires, the Persian forces were vast, with contingents from across the Persian Empire. There were perhaps over 316,000 men, though many of

the number were not soldiers, for the whole of the royal court had come along with wives, children, concubines, musicians, administrators, cooks, servants and slaves of every description.

Darius himself was at the heart of it, seated in his resplendent gold chariot, draped in his royal cloak, with spear and shield in hand as if he were the sun god himself, surrounded by the cream of his army, the archers of the Royal Guard. These were the Immortals, 10,000 of them, spoken of with awe and dread, because when any one of them fell, another appeared in his place.

So confident was Darius of victory, that he had not only brought along his treasures and wealth, but also his mother, wife, two of his daughters and his young son to witness the battle.

He had created a front line with his royal bodyguards which was 2,000 strong in the centre. On either side was a heavily armed cavalry made up of about 30,000 Greek mercenaries. On the wings, he had deployed two divisions of light-armed Persian infantry – young men who were barely out of training.

It was mid afternoon. The Persians were in position. Alexander showed no impatience. He moved down from the hills at a leisurely pace, with frequent halts to rest his soldiers and check the enemy's movements. He had calculated that King Darius would attack him on the right wing. But with sudden surprise, there was a swift movement of Persian cavalry, and a surge to the left. A tight phalanx of Darius' forces were attacking Parmenion on the seashore.

Alexander had to think quickly and change his tactics. He was being assailed on all sides. There were enemies to his left, and others coming up behind him to the right. He ordered a contingent of Thessalians to

reinforce Parmenion, instructing them to ride unnoticed behind his infantry and their wall of sarissas, and sent lightly-armed commandos into the hills to deal with a ragtag of inexperienced Persians who were occupying a spur of a mountain behind them.

Forming a three-mile front, Alexander's army continued to move forwards. The vast forces of the Persian army glittered before them. The Macedonians halted out of bow-shot. Alexander hoped the Persians would be tempted to charge, but they didn't. There was nothing for it but to continue the advance into arrow range.

The Persian archers fired first. A ferocious volley of arrows hissed over the river into the Macedonians. A trumpet sounded. Alexander's men charged across the river, driving back the Persian archers and scattering them among the light infantry. But it was messy. The soldiers struggled in the river, and the phalanx fell into disarray. Darius saw that Alexander's charge had weakened his centre, so he attacked in the middle, driving a deep wedge into it. It was a brief victory. 120 Macedonians were killed, including Ptolemy, son of Seleucus.

Once across the river, Alexander pulled the wedge of his cavalry together and, urging his men onwards with huge ferocity, he swung the wedge into the centre. The target was the Great King Darius himself. If he could be killed or captured, it would not only change the course of the battle but weaken the entire Persian Empire.

There was the royal ornamental chariot, and Darius in the midst of his bodyguards, the Immortals, in their amazing robes of gold brocade, with gold collars and long-sleeved tunics studded with gems — as if they could dazzle their enemies and prove that they were indeed immortal.

But Alexander not only created myths, he smashed them too. The Immortals were only too mortal. Once again, it was Alexander's manoeuvrability which made him so lethal. Mounted on his beloved Bucephalus, he wheeled and turned, pitched and thrust, plunging nearer and nearer to the king. The fight was desperate. There was a confusion of men and horses, struggling and dying. Alexander was wounded in the thigh. Darius' chariot was being carried closer and closer into Alexander's lines. His brother Oxathres tried desperately to protect him. Darius himself grabbed the reins of his chariot and attempted to extricate himself, but it was no use. In the heat of battle, Darius and Alexander stared each other in the face, eyeball to eyeball.

Then the Great King's nerve broke. Darius had always been portrayed as the great horseman, archer and warrior, but when he saw defeat was inevitable, he sprang from his chariot into another which had been brought up alongside, and fled, abandoning his men, his mother, wife and children. Confused and panicked, some of his army followed him, but the rest — thousands of them — crumbled and fled in all directions; into the river, into the sea, into the hills; some were trampled underfoot, while others plunged over precipices.

Alexander went in hot pursuit, and chased the Persian king for 25 miles, deep into the mountains. If only he could capture him, his victory would be complete. Frantically, Darius abandoned the chariot for a horse, and flung off his royal cloak and insignia, his shield and bow, all to be gathered up by Alexander.

Night was falling. It was clear that Darius had escaped.

Alexander knew he could go no further. Though the king had got

away, Alexander could triumphantly sport Darius' royal cloak, shield and insignia, and he had possession of the considerable spoils of Issus, which he badly needed to fund his army. Most importantly of all, his biggest prize was Darius' family: his mother, his wife, who many said was the fairest in all Asia, their two daughters and their son. Priceless hostages.

Dusty and exhausted, Alexander returned to his camp — at least to enjoy the spoils of war. Tonight he would sleep in Darius' sumptuous royal tent with its gold and silver inlaid furniture, and bathe away the dust of war in the extraordinary royal bathtub. "So this is how a king lives!" exclaimed Alexander with relish.

As food was being served to Alexander on the royal gold and silver tableware, the sound of wailings and lamentations reached his ears. He paused in his eating and asked what the noise was about. "It is Darius' family, his mother, wife and children," they told Alexander. "They have seen the Great King's cloak and shield, and believe him to be dead."

Alexander had them brought before him.

The two queens and the children entered the royal tent. They knew anything was possible. They could be humiliated, enslaved or killed. Darius' mother, Queen Sisygambis, saw two noblemen, both handsome, both dressed the same but one taller than the other. Thinking the taller man to be Alexander, she prostrated herself before him.

THE HOSTAGE QUEEN

"No, no!" She heard whispers, sniggers, shock, for she had fallen before Hephaistion, Alexander's best friend. Disconcerted and confused, she tried to bow before Alexander, apologizing for her mistake, but he said with a kind smile, "Fear not, Mother, he too is Alexander."

So the Battle of Issus was over. A letter came from the runaway king, Darius, begging for the return of his family. Alexander rejected his request and added scornfully, "From now on, when you have occasion to address me, do so as the King of Asia. Do not write as equal to equal."

Although Alexander refused to release the family, and ignored all peace overtures from Darius, he treated his royal prisoners with the greatest respect, and Queen Sisygambis became one of his closest friends and confidantes.

After Issus, Alexander marched down the Phoenecian coast. Town after town fell or surrendered. Many had disliked the savagery of some of their Persian rulers. Tripolis, Byblos and Sidon yielded fairly peacefully, and Tyre was next.

Chapter Eight

THE SIEGE OF TYRE

Tyre meant a lot to Alexander; not just because it was an important and strategic port, but because here was one of the most ancient temples to the demi-god, Heracles, who the Tyrians called Melkart and to whom Alexander claimed to be related. The town was surrounded by rich pastures, where the finest quality cattle roamed – like the divine herd of Geryones, which Heracles had been ordered to capture as one of his Twelve Labours.

THE TWELVE LABOURS OF HERACLES

 Heracles, who the Romans later called Hercules – half god, half human son of Zeus, born of Alcmene, a human princess – was loathed by a jealous goddess, Hera, wife of Zeus, who was determined to destroy

him. But Heracles had been endowed with a colossal strength and, even as a babe in his cradle, fought off two monstrous serpents that she sent to crush him to death. When Heracles had completed his education with Chiron, the Centaur, and was at last a man, he set out into the world, still pursued by the vengeful Hera.

One day, Hera caused him to be seized by madness and, in a fit of delirium, he killed his wife and children. His punishment was to serve the evil Eurystheus, his wicked cousin.

Eurystheus demanded the impossible of Heracles and set him twelve tasks, any of which could bring about Heracles' destruction. But whether it was slaying a monstrous lion, or the many-headed serpent, Hydra, or whether it was fighting the loathsome giant, Cacus, for the divine cattle of Geryon, Heracles finally succeeded in overcoming all his labours.

But was not jealousy the start of all his troubles? Jealousy would also be the cause of his downfall. Heracles had saved the beautiful Deianeira during one of his labours and had married her. When he left her to continue on his way across the world, completing his labours, she had been given a special garment by the lustful centaur Nessus, who had tried to make off with her. This present of repentance was supposed to have magic powers. Nessus told her that if she ever felt Heracles no longer loved her, she should ask him to wear this garment, and all his love would return.

On his way home, Heracles stopped at the court of Eurytus, where he beheld the maid, Iole. He had first met her when they were children, and he had loved her then. Now, she was still young, and he realized he still loved her. How hard he found it to leave. Day by day, he lingered on in the court, just to be near her.

Deianeira heard rumours, and was desperate to keep her husband. At last she heard he was on his way home, but bringing Iole with him. She took out the magic garment and gave it to a messenger. "Deliver this to Heracles," she ordered, "and beg him to wear it."

The messenger delivered the garment. It was a wondrous glittering thing, and when Heracles saw it, he couldn't resist putting it on.

But the wicked centaur, Nessus, had cheated Deianeira. The garment would not restore Heracles' love, for it was laced with poison, and the moment Heracles put it on, the poison enveloped his body like fire.

Wracked with agony, Heracles despaired that he would never be free from the torments of this world. He ordered his servants to build his funeral pyre, but they couldn't bring themselves to do it, and begged him to live. No amount of entreaties could make him change his mind, and when they wouldn't build his pyre, Heracles climbed a mountain, tore out huge oaks from their roots, and made his own funeral pyre. Then he laid down his pain-racked body, and asked his best friend, Philoctetes, to light the pyre.

As the flames rose, Zeus came down to clasp his son's mighty soul in his arms, and bore him away to dwell with the gods on Mount Olympus.

So the Tyre of Heracles meant a lot to Alexander, and he was determined to have it. Taking first the diplomatic route, he sent an emissary to the city asking if he could sacrifice at the Temple of Melkart.

For the Tyrians to allow Alexander this favour would be in effect to acknowledge him as their ruler, for only kings and priests were allowed

to sacrifice in the temple. The people of Tyre had no intention of letting Alexander take the most strategic port of all. They were proud, with a fine navy and much wealth. They were willing to welcome Alexander as a guest into their city, but announced their neutrality, unwilling that either a Persian or a Macedonian should take them over. "After all," they said, "we don't yet know who the winner will be." And they killed Alexander's emissary.

Alexander was furious, and immediately declared war on the city.

While Alexander prepares for battle, hear now of the glories of Tyre; listen to stories going back as far as the creation of the world.

THE AMBROSIAL ROCKS

In the beginning, when the people of Tyre had just begun to build their city on the edge of the sea, they had very little room to expand. Just a little way offshore into the sea were two rocks known as the Ambrosial Rocks. The citizens longed to be able to extend their city and build on the rocks too. But they were unstable, often floating up and down with the waves. The seers had said that an eagle must be sacrificed to make the rocks stable.

So the first man, Ousos, sailed to the rocks where, perched on top of an olive tree, was an eagle. However, coiled round the trunk was a deadly serpent which prevented Ousos from getting onto the rocks so that

he could kill the eagle. The eagle, understanding why Ousos had come, offered itself as a sacrifice, and immediately the rocks became stable.

The citizens of Tyre extended their city by building on the rocks and, for many years, Tyre was in two parts, divided by the sea. The city grew and grew, and the god they worshipped was Melkart.

Every time you look at a rainbow, remember Melkart, the god of Tyre. Every time you see the colour purple, think of kings, think of power, think of gods, think of Tyre! For this is how the colour purple was discovered.

One day, Melkart was strolling along the seashore with his beloved, the sea nymph, Tyrus. Their dog, who had been chasing the waves, suddenly came bounding towards them, and they were horrified to see his mouth dripping with blood. But when the dog came close, they realized it wasn't blood, but some substance dripping from a shell, which he held in his jaws. It was a Murex shell. Tyrus gasped at the sight of such a beautiful colour — such as had only ever been seen in the rainbow. If only she could have a dress of that colour.

So Melkart gathered hundreds of Murex shells. When he had enough, he extracted the colour purple and dyed cloth, out of which a beautiful robe was made for his dearest Tyrus. From then on, purple became the colour of royalty.

In 980 BC King Hiram came to the throne.

One day, he had a dream. His dream was to build the finest city in the world, with temples and palaces. But his first plan was to fill in the sea between the rocks and the land, to link the two parts of Tyre and create one marvellous city. With sand and rubble, he filled in the gap and soon a causeway was created linking the two.

Then he set about fulfilling his dream. First he built a dazzling temple of cedar wood, with pillars of gold and emeralds, and dedicated it to Melkart, the protector of sailors and merchants. It was so magnificent, even King Solomon, in Jerusalem, asked King Hiram to help him build his own temple.

Then King Hiram set about creating the greatest and most beautiful city in Phoenicia. Because he was still short of land, Hiram built tall. His buildings were three or four storeys high. Tyre's fame spread.

And many people came to worship at the temple and marvel at the city.

By the time Alexander came to Tyre, the causeway built by King Hiram had sunk long ago, and the city was once more divided into two parts.

Alexander surrounded the city and besieged it. Then he brought in engineers to build the causeway again and link the rocky island back to the mainland. He had siege towers built — some floating on water — and turned the vast walls of the city, which were 150 feet high, into the walls of a prison, trapping the Tyrians in their own city. All round the outside, he deployed siege engines and battering rams, catapults and sling-throwers. The Tyrians responded with flaming arrows, blocks of stone and burning hot sand which rained down on Alexander's troops from the battlements, and they sent secret underwater swimmers, who attempted to destroy the causeway. The battle was bitter; the Tyrians were stubborn and valiant, and the siege lasted seven whole months.

The seers and soothsayers were kept busy with their predictions.

A bird flying overhead dropped a stone which landed on Alexander's helmet. Although he was unhurt, he consulted a seer to interpret the omen. "You will take the city today," pronounced the seer. "But watch out for your safety."

Never one to listen to soothsayers unless it suited him, Alexander plunged back into commanding the battle, pitching himself into the fray, dodging knives and arrows, till finally he was struck by a bolt from an enemy crossbow.

The seer was right. Though bleeding heavily, Alexander fought on until he fainted. Drifting in and out of consciousness, he continued to direct the battle till the city fell, and entered as victor. But the losses had been huge, the bloodshed appalling. 3,500 citizens were slaughtered or enslaved.

Alexander went to the temple and performed sacrifices to Melkart, his supposed ancestor, though one historian commented wryly: "Never had this god received such a blood-stained sacrifice."

Darius had fled the field of Issus ignominiously. But he was not beaten yet. He was gathering his army and his mighty fleet back together again, and Alexander knew that not only must Tyre be won (and held) but so too must all the other ports on the way to Egypt.

Having defeated Tyre, Alexander charged on down the coast and took Gaza, very much a Persian stronghold. It too put up strong resistance. It was strongly fortified and occupied by Arabs and Persians. The battle was bloody but short-lived, and soon, a victorious Alexander was on his way to Egypt.

Darius, The Great King, sent more messages calling for a truce. He offered Alexander the sum of 10,000 talents for the return of his family, and promised him all Asia Minor west of the Euphrates, as well as his daughter's hand in marriage.

Alexander's senior general, Parmenion said, "If I were Alexander I would accept the truce and end the war without any further risk." Alexander is said to have replied, "If I were Parmenion, so would I," and he rejected the offers.

CHAPTER NINE

INTO EGYPT

Alexander and his army have crossed the treacherous deserts and marshlands and arrived in Memphis, the capital of the Upper Nile in the Land of the Pharaohs.

Egypt had been conquered by the Persian king, Artaxerxes III, eleven years earlier. But the Egyptians had hated Artaxerxes. They had called him The Sword, because of his brutal repression of them, and accused him of killing, roasting and eating the sacred bull of their god, Apis. So when in 332 BC Alexander and his army rode down the Phoenician coast towards Egypt, city after city flung open their gates and hailed them as heroes. Memphis welcomed him not as a conqueror, but as a redeemer, and the Egyptians ran before his chariot strewing his path with flowers.

This was one of the most ancient civilizations in the world, older even than Greece, and Alexander and his followers knew the names and the stories.

Ah men, Ra, Tut, Khnum, Shu! These were the names of early Egyptian gods. But it was long, long ago, when the land was inhabited by broken tribes, wandering like savages, fighting each other in the valleys and among the hills, that the tales of Isis and Osiris were first told.

OSIRIS AND ISIS

Osiris came down from heaven with his wife Isis. When he was born on earth as a human, a voice from heaven proclaimed, "Here cometh the Lord of All Things," and a wise man in Thebes told all the people to rejoice, because a good and noble king had appeared among them.

Osiris introduced agriculture. He taught men to make tools to help them break up the land, sew the seeds, reap the harvest and produce corn and flour. He planted fruit trees and trained the vine. He made laws, proclaimed decrees and sat in wise judgement. He had a message which he carried all over his kingdom, that peace was better than war.

Isis the Strong taught many skills: how to weave cloth, spin flax, make bread out of wheat, and grind corn. She had magic powers of healing, and was a goddess of medicine and wisdom.

When Osiris went away to administer his other territories, he left his consort, Isis, in charge of the kingdom.

But Osiris had a brother called Seth, who was jealous and tried to stir up trouble. He waited till Osiris had left the capital on a tour of the land, and then conspired to destroy him.

A royal feast was prepared to welcome Osiris back to the palace. Seth came to the feast with his conspirators, and brought with him a magnificent chest — all beautifully carved and decorated — but which Seth had secretly ordered to be made exactly to the measurements of Osiris' body.

It was such a magnificent piece of work that everyone admired it and wished it was theirs. Seth said, if there were a man whose body fitted into the chest, then he could have it.

There was much merriment and banter as, one by one, men climbed into the chest to see if they fitted in. Soon every guest had tried — and not one of them fitted exactly. Then Osiris came forward — so innocently, so full of the joys of the feast, and the warm friendship he felt around him. He climbed into the chest — and he fitted it perfectly.

But even as he called out in triumph, Seth's evil followers leaped forward and slammed down the lid of the chest. They hammered it tight with nails and sealed it with lead. The chest became a coffin. The feast became a battleground; blood flowed and confusion spread. In the mayhem, Seth had the coffin smuggled away. No one saw the evil men take it to the banks of the River Nile and cast it in. No one saw it carried away by the currents. All they knew was that the reign of Osiris had ended, and Seth with his evil and tyrannical ways would now rule.

Isis was grief-stricken. She cut off her hair and made a vow that she would not rest untill she had found the chest containing Osiris. Even though she was pregnant, she put on garments of mourning, and set off on her quest.

Far and wide she wandered, asking all she met if any had seen this chest.

But each time they shook their heads sadly and could tell her nothing.

She became a fugitive, having to hide from her enemies in swamps and jungles. The god Ra looked down on her with pity. He sent seven giant scorpions to protect her.

One day, she came to the wild marshlands near the mouth of the Nile before it opened into the sea. As she wandered along a lonely shore, she came across some children. They had seen a chest, they cried. It had floated down the Nile and had drifted into the sea near the city of Tanis.

By now, Isis knew that her baby was due to be born and she needed shelter. One evening she came to the dwelling of a poor woman. At her knock, the woman opened the door. However, at the sight of the seven scorpions, she slammed the door shut in terror. As a punishment, one of the scorpions gained entry and stung the poor woman's child, who then died. Screams of lamentation came from the distraught mother. Isis took pity and, murmuring magical words, brought the child back to life. Filled with gratitude and remorse, the poor woman welcomed the wandering queen into her house.

Isis lived there in safety until she gave birth to a son called Horus. However, Seth came to know about the birth of this boy child and, fearing that the son of Osiris might one day claim the throne, he sent out his men to find and kill the child. But up in heaven, the god Thoth warned Isis in time and she fled the house with her child.

Isis came to the city of Buto where there was a virgin goddess who was also a serpent. Her name was Uazit. Isis entrusted her beloved son to the virgin goddess, who promised to take care of him, then continued her search for the chest.

Meanwhile, as the children had told her, the chest had floated out of the mouth of the Nile into the sea, where it was at last cast upon a Syrian shore near the town of Byblos. A marvellous tree had sprung up around it and enveloped the chest with its twisting branches. The king of that land was amazed. He ordered the tree to be cut down and had the trunk, to which the chest was sealed, erected as a pillar inside his palace for all to see. No one knew, though, what was in the chest.

Isis had a dream. It told her to go by sea to the shore near Byblos. Dressed as a common villager, she left the ship and wandered into the town. She came to a well and sat there weeping. Many women approached her with concern, but she didn't cease from weeping until the royal handmaidens also came to see what was happening. They spoke to her gently and offered her help.

Isis thanked them for their kindness and offered to braid their hair. As each one's hair was plaited, Isis breathed into the hair, so that they returned to the palace sweetly perfumed. The queen asked why they smelled so sweet, and they told her about the strange woman. The queen sent for Isis.

Isis, the queen-goddess revealed who she really was and asked the king for the sacred pillar. The king agreed, and Isis cut deep into the trunk and brought out the coffin which had been sealed inside. It was taken to her ship, and Isis set sail for Egypt, carrying home, at last, the body of her dead husband.

When she reached Egypt, she hid the chest in a forest, and hurried longingly to find her son, Horus. But alas, Seth was out hunting boar that night and, by the light of the moon, he came across the hidden chest. He opened it to find the body of Osiris. The body was taken out and Seth commanded that it be chopped up into fourteen pieces and thrown to the crocodiles in the Nile. However, the crocodiles feared the wrath of Isis and would not eat the pieces of Osiris, so when Isis heard what had taken place, once more she went out in search of her husband's remains. She made herself a boat out of papyrus and sailed up and down until she had collected every piece. Then all along the banks of the Nile, she buried him, fragment by fragment, weeping and wailing, and built a temple over each one.

Once again, Ra heard her lamentations and sent down Anubis, the jackal-headed god of embalming, to help her. They assembled all the pieces of the body of Osiris and wrapped them in linen bandages.

Isis was transformed, becoming winged and, as a goddess once more, hovered over his body and breathed life into his nostrils. And so Osiris lived again as man and god. He became Judge and King of the Dead.

Before he set out on his conquest, Alexander had reached and crossed one of the greatest rivers in Europe, the Danube. Here he was on the edge of Africa, on the banks of another great river, the Nile – a legendary river about which he had heard so many stories when he was a child.

Now he could marvel himself at its fertile lands, towering temples, the extraordinary pyramids and the great sphinx in the desert. Nothing he had ever seen in his life could have prepared him for the wonders of Egypt.

His first act was to worship at the shrine of Apis, the Bull, and offer sacrifices. How different from the previous conqueror, the Persian Ochus who, like Ataxerxes, had deliberately slaughtered a sacred bull and ordered it to be roasted for dinner.

Alexander was hailed as a Deliverer, and enthroned as Pharaoh. They gave him the symbols of the Shepherd and the Judge. They called him Horus, the Strong Prince, beloved of Amun, Selected of Ra, Son of Ra, Alexandros. They had made him not just a king, but according to their traditions, a god.

As Alexander moved from kingdom to kingdom, country to country, from one religion to another, he knew he could rule more effectively if he, as emperor, was also seen to be a god, so he accepted the aspect of a god of Egypt. If in Greece he was known as the son of Zeus, related to Heracles and Dionyses, in Egypt, he happily took on the title, Son of Amun, for Amun, the ram-headed god, was also known as Zeus Ammon.

Endowed with such power and respect, Alexander took a boat from Memphis and sailed down the Nile to the coast to explore the Nile Delta and visit the Pharaoh's fort at Rhacotis. It was the year 331 BC.

THE FOUNDING OF ALEXANDRIA

Where the Nile met the sea, there was a natural harbour around the fort, on the western edge of the delta. It struck Alexander as an ideal site for building a city port.

Excitedly, he walked over the area, explaining his vision to the architects and engineers, describing in detail where everything should be: here the market place, here gathering spaces for the people, here the temples dedicated to both Egyptian gods and Greek, and here the perimeter walls. His followers ran alongside, trying to record his thoughts.

He had no chalk to mark out his dimensions, so he used meal which someone resourcefully thought of. But as he sprinkled it, birds came down and ate it. Wondering what this omen meant, Alexander anxiously consulted the seers. They reassured him it meant that he would build a flourishing city which would feed everyone.

Fantastical tales were told of monsters in the sea which tried to prevent Alexander from building his city, so Alexander built and entered a glass chest which was lowered under the waves. He descended to the bottom of the ocean so that he could draw these terrible creatures, and when he resurfaced, he had huge images made in metal, which lined the buildings along the sea front. When the monsters surfaced from the depths and saw their own images, they turned and fled away.

Whatever the stories, Alexander built his Egyptian city and called it Alexandria. It was one of the most modern and technologically advanced cities in the world, with roads and bridges, temples and palaces, and an intricate and effective system of water delivery throughout the city.

This pearl of the Mediterranean, situated at the heart of three great continents, Europe, Asia and Africa, reached its glorious apex, after Alexander's death, when his general Ptolemy became Pharaoh. Ptolemy built both the glorious Great Library, which celebrated scholarship, and was a storehouse of learning throughout the known world, and the Pharos Lighthouse — one of the Seven Wonders of the World. It was the first lighthouse ever. With its giant mirror, it not only guided ships but also, it was said, could set enemy fleets on fire with its powerful reflector.

But the vision was Alexander's. Perhaps he was still trying to prove himself to the Greeks: that he was as civilized, as cultured and as literate as any of them. Perhaps he had wanted Alexandria to rival Athens as a seat of learning and power. Of all his exploits, whether he was thought to be a great leader, or just a power-mad, genocidal maniac, Alexandria would be his finest legacy. It would be recognized as one of the seven ancient Wonders of the World.

Ra, Ah, Ptah, Anubis, Mut or Nekhebet, Horus, Isis and Osiris. How strange the names must have sounded to Alexander and his men. And what new sights they saw too: the pyramids in the desert, and the astonishing sphinx gazing out across the sands. Some saw crocodiles for the first time, and learned about incredible beasts like the hippopotamus; they heard of magic serpents, sacred cats, gods with the head of an eagle or a dog.

But it was Ammon who Alexander thought about in the depths of his soul. Zeus Ammon.

It was Alexander's father, Philip, who said that to keep power, one must also be worshipped as a god. Alexander wondered if he was really the son of Zeus. Was he a god? He could proclaim himself as a god, but he needed proof. Being a god meant more to Alexander than just being a means of holding on to power. He wanted to find a single source of truth for himself — something that told him who he really was.

As a Macedonian, he would never be truly accepted by the Greeks. Even though his whole education and philosophical thinking had been shaped by Aristotle, Plato, Socrates and the great Greek dramatists, to the Athenians he would always be an outsider. But he found a spiritual home in Egypt.

Alexander's mother had told him he was the son of Zeus. Perhaps here in Egypt he could find out if that was really true. He had so many inner

questions. Were there answers to these questions?

He had heard of the oasis at Siwa, where there was an oracle dedicated to Ammon. It was three hundred miles across an expanse of desolate and uninhabited desert on the borders between Egypt and Libya. Hardly anyone went there — it was too far into a pitiless desert, and anyway, no one else thought it important.

Who can guess why Alexander was gripped with such a longing to visit this shrine? According to legend, Perseus and Heracles were supposed to have consulted the oracle at Siwa. Did Alexander want to link himself with these heroic gods and heroes?

It must have been a deeply profound craving that sent Alexander on this long seventeen-day trek into the desert. Even though news was coming in that Darius was once again mobilizing his troops, he said he must go to the Oracle. Risking everything, including his life, he set off for the oasis of Siwa. The journey itself became a myth.

A southerly wind buried the track across the desert; it was as desolate as the open sea, with no mark, tree, hill or track to show them the way. The guides were bewildered and lost their bearings, and Alexander and his men were in danger of going dangerously astray. Suddenly, two hissing snakes appeared before them. With nothing to lose, Alexander said, "Follow them." The snakes led them all the way to the Oracle.

THE ORACLE
AT SIWA

Siwa is a miracle, surrounded as it is on all sides by waterless barren desert. It is a small oasis of fruit trees and olive trees, where large crystals of mineral salt can be gathered, where dew falls, and where the temple stands at the source of a spring running with sweet water.

As Alexander approached the temple, a priest came out and hailed him as Pharaoh, son of Zeus Ammon. Alexander entered the temple alone. He said he had a question to ask the Oracle, but told no one what that question was, and when he came out of the temple, no one knew what he had been told.

Did he ask, "Am I the son of Ammon?"

Did the Oracle reply, "Yes"?

No one knows. Alexander said only that he had received the answer his soul desired, and it was clear that he had undergone a mystical experience which, from that day on, affected his life to the end.

CHAPTER TEN

CROSSING THE TIGRIS

Now, with confidence, Alexander claimed to be the successor and son of Zeus and disowned his father Philip. Coins were minted depicting him with ram's horns which are the symbol of Ammon. But for the early Persians, these were the horns of the devil. They called him Iskander Dhulkarnein, Alexander the Two-Horned, Alexander The Damned.

Since Alexander had crossed the Hellespont three years previously, to defeat the Persians and conquer Asia, he had not just been pounding from one battle to the next. In between, there was the day to day need to administrate his newly conquered lands. He spent a year in Egypt after his visit to the oasis at Siwa.

But though Alexander felt that Egypt was his spiritual home, he knew he must leave if he was to fulfil his goal of overcoming Darius. The ancient city of Babylon must be the next prize.

As for Darius, he had, in the meantime, been reassembling his forces. Alexander had to be stopped. It was unthinkable that he should conquer

Babylon which was at the heart of Darius' commercial empire. If he took Babylon, next would be Persia itself – and the glorious palaces of Susa and Persepolis.

Desperately, Darius went to every corner of his empire to raise his army; horsemen from Bactria, mounted archers from Scythia, elephant-mounted troops from India. There were Arachosians, Arians, Parthians, Babylonians, Armenians, Syrians and Cappadocians as well as Greek mercenaries. He had 40,000 cavalry, 100,000 infantry and 200 horse-drawn scythed chariots with iron-pointed spears protruding in front, three-sword blades on either side of the yokes, javelin points stuck outwards from the wheels, and scythe blades fixed to the rims of the wheels, which mowed down everything they passed.

Then he let Alexander know that he was ready for battle.

Alexander had returned to Tyre, and stationed himself there, dealing with administrative matters, trying to consolidate the cities and towns already conquered. However, when the call to battle came, although the summer heat was still intense, Alexander had to respond, or lose all he had gained. With his far smaller army of only 47,000, he set off across the burning desert wastes into Mesopotamia.

There were stories about how they got hopelessly lost, and began to fear they would die of thirst, when two crows came to their rescue, cawing to round up stragglers, and flying ahead until they were back on track again.

This made Alexander and his men feel that the gods were on their side, for of all living creatures, birds were especially respected because they could fly higher than any other living thing, and so were the link between

men on the ground and the gods in their heavens. Birds had special powers, and were messengers, portents and bringers of good and evil. They carried gods and heroes on their backs.

There were many stories about Alexander and birds: how he ascended into the sky on the back of an eagle, so that he could see what the whole world looked like. How, from on high, he saw the length and breadth of the earth, and understood that to conquer Asia, he must cross many mountains, rivers and seas.

They said he flew to the very heights of heaven and explored them too, then descended into the Country of Darkness where he fed and tamed giant birds – even larger than eagles; that he ordered four of his soldiers to mount these giant birds, which carried them off to the "Land of the Living". When the soldiers returned, they told Alexander about everything they had seen.

Heading now for Babylon, he would have examined all the omens, consulted his seers and fervently performed all his religious duties as, yet again, he braced himself for another encounter with Darius.

Darius had two strong generals, Mazaeus and Bessus. After losing the whole of Asia Minor and Egypt to the young Macedonian, and especially after the humiliating defeat they had incurred at Issus, they wanted a watertight plan of action. They decided to lure Alexander to a battlefield of their choosing, where they would be fully prepared finally to put an end to his ambitions.

There were really only two ways to approach Babylon and Darius wanted to defend both of them – but if possible to force Alexander to take the longer and more difficult route. Whichever way he went, both routes

would eventually lead Alexander and his men to a plain in Gaugamela.

With Babylon as the next major goal, Darius knew that Alexander would head for the River Euphrates, and the main crossing point at the town of Thapsacus. There he would be faced with a choice: either to cross the Euphrates and head southwards along the river directly for Babylon, or to turn left along the Euphrates, then leaving it behind, to march north eastwards across the barren unfriendly wastes of the Mesopotamian plain to the River Tigris beyond. Then he would have to cross this far more dangerous river before turning southwards towards Babylon.

All things being equal, Darius was sure Alexander would want the quickest route down the fertile banks of the Euphrates to Babylon. In anticipation of him choosing this option, Darius's general, Mazaeus, planned to carry out a scorched earth policy, so that when Alexander arrived at Thapsacus, he would be forced to take the northerly route.

Alexander arrived on the banks of the River Euphrates. His engineers had already gone on ahead and built a pontoon bridge for the crossing. Strangely, they were unopposed, apart from a few skirmishes, and taunts thrown at each other across the river. Instead of attacking, Mazaeus disappeared with his men down the south-easterly banks of the Euphrates, burning and destroying all possible food sources for Alexander's army.

So far, the Persian plan was working. Alexander didn't take the scorched earth route, and to cross the wasteland directly ahead was unthinkable. So, after crossing the Euphrates, he turned away northwards towards the cooler, more fertile land beneath the Armenian mountains, heading towards the upper ground between the Euphrates and the Tigris.

He took five weeks. The army had food and supplies, and the scorching heat was less intense as they made their way to the rushing Tigris River.

Darius could have been lying in wait there too. The river was fierce and dangerous and would be difficult to cross. But even though spies had told Alexander that the Persian army was nearby, and he was expecting trouble, when they arrived, there was no Great King, no huge army, and Alexander crossed virtually unopposed.

Was it the Great King's incompetence or was it over confidence? After all, he too felt godlike; he too was an Appointed One, the god of the Persians, Ahura Mazda. Darius may have felt that a battle here was too small, and that he must fight Alexander on a bigger scale. He would want to win a major and more decisive battle for all to see, where he could wash away the memory of his earlier defeats, and especially his flight from the field at Issus.

So, on 19 September 331 BC, Alexander's men crossed the treacherous Tigris River and camped.

CROSSING THE
TIGRIS

They were deep in enemy territory. Fear permeated the ranks. The terror was increased almost to breaking point when, on the night of 20 September there was a total eclipse of the moon. Surely the gods were angry? Eclipses were always a sign of the gods' displeasure.

Alexander made elaborate sacrifices to the Sun, Moon and Earth. The hills and valleys glowed with sacrificial fires, and rang with the sounds of clashing cymbals, beating drums and the voices of singers. His seer, Aristander, reassured the men that these ceremonies had pleased the gods. The failure of the moon to appear, he told them, meant that the power of

the Persians would be eclipsed, and the battle would be fought before the month was out.

The panicky troops were comforted. The next day, still not pressing his men hard, Alexander led them at a gentle pace, until they picked up the Royal Road to Babylon.

What Alexander didn't know then was that Darius had selected a battleground about 76 miles away to the south. The Great King didn't want to make the same mistake as he had at Issus, where he had abandoned the wide plain. This time the Persian armies converged on open land at Gaugamela, near the river Bumodus, and there Darius was already preparing the rough ground, levelling it off to make it easier for his war chariots.

CHAPTER ELEVEN

THE BATTLE OF GAUGAMELA

It is 25 September. Scouts have reported seeing Persian troops only seven miles away. Alexander pauses and sets up a base camp for all the camp followers – which also include Darius' family: his wife, his mother-in-law and his children. He dallies, to give himself time to think, and to keep the enemy guessing; keep them nervously on their toes till they lose their high peak of concentration. As usual, he is intently focused, making sure that his troops have checked their equipment and groomed their horses.

Four days later, Alexander amassed his troops and set off through the night, meaning to attack at daybreak. Four miles from the battleground, they reached a ridge and looked down on the plain, glimmering with thousands of enemy campfires. It was a shock, even for Alexander. Where Darius had an army of at least 245,000, he had only about 47,000.

The Persians were an awesome sight. Alexander's troops were terror-stricken and on the edge of panic. He knew he had lost the element of

surprise for the moment and drew back, forcing his men to lay down their arms and rest easy. Then he undertook a series of rituals, prayer and oblations.

A terrible sense of foreboding and despair hung over the troops; a disbelief that even Alexander could overcome such forces.

Only something extraordinary could help them. For the first, and only, time in his whole life, Alexander sacrificed a human victim. Perhaps he felt it was the only act that could placate and soothe his frightened soldiers, and put courage back into the hearts of his men, many of whom came from different faiths and nationalities.

Perhaps he thought back to Homer's Troy, to those Greek heroes, Odysseus, Ajax and his beloved Achilles, and to how, before they set sail against the Trojans, King Agamemnon sacrificed his own daughter, Iphigenia, to Poseidon, beseeching him to lead them to victory.

The next day, showing that he had not lost his nerve, Alexander calmly went on a detailed reconnaissance. With a group of Companions, he examined the whole area. Darius' troops were already in battle formation, forewarned by his spies that Alexander was near.

The Persians saw him going round, making minute notes of where they had set stakes and snares designed to tear into his cavalry, and where they had levelled the ground. But they did nothing. This must be a battle won openly and decisively.

Alexander returned to his fearful troops to restore their confidence.

It was one of the great speeches of his life.

"I don't need to remind you of your duty!" he said. "Remember all our past battles, our victories, our acts of heroism. I don't need to

beg you to be brave, you are already brave. All I ask is that every single one of you, no matter what your rank, whether you are a commander of a company, a squadron, a brigade, or a lowly infantryman, must be responsible for absolute discipline. Orders must be obeyed instantly in this hour of danger; advance when ordered, maintain utter silence when needed, and wait for the moment to give the battle-cry, when you can put the fear of god into the hearts of the enemy. On the conduct of each one of you depends the fate of us all. If any one of you neglects your duty, the whole army will fall, but if each man plays his part, we will win."

His senior general, Parmenion, and all the other generals, advised Alexander to attack the Persians by night, but Alexander retorted, "Alexander does not steal his victories like a thief."

This was not just a stubborn quip. Alexander already knew that it would be dangerous for his troops to attack by night – for the most dangerous risk in battle was confusion. Perhaps he also knew that this battle above all would represent the decisive moment when he could finally rout Darius, and take possession of the Persian Empire – and this he wanted to do in full daylight, for all to see. So he dismissed his generals, telling them they would go into attack at dawn.

He ordered that the men be well fed, then he sent them to bed for a good night's rest.

But Alexander didn't go to bed. Because of his detailed reconnaissance, he knew exactly what Darius' battle plan would be. He sat up long into the night plotting his strategies and working out his course of action.

The dawn of 1 October broke. The camp stirred. The generals

prepared their men. But Alexander slept. The sun rose higher — and still he slept. The officers went to his tent to wake him, and found him sleeping like a babe. They were amazed. "How can you sleep as if the battle were already won?" they cried.

"Do you think this battle is not already won," smiled Alexander, "now that we have been spared having to chase Darius, who burns his earth and fights by retreating?"

He dressed for battle. He is described as wearing a shirt woven in Sicily. His breastplate was a double thickness of linen, taken as spoil at Issus. His iron helmet made by the silversmith, Theophilis, gleamed like pure silver, while his neck-piece iron, made of iron and studded with precious stones, fitted him closely. His sword was amazingly light and well-tempered, a present from a Cypriot king, and he also sported a cloak, more elaborately worked than the rest of his armour. It had been dyed by Helicon, the famous weaver of Cyprus, and given to him by the city of Rhodes.

Mounted on his beloved horse, Bucephalus, he toured his troops, rousing them to battle with calls to the gods, reminding them of his own special kinship with Zeus Ammon. To emphasize the link, his seer, Aristander, pointed out an eagle flying high overhead — a symbol of Zeus — an omen that god was on their side.

At last, towards midday, Alexander finally led his men — all 47,000 of them — down towards the battlefield to face the overwhelming might of Darius' army.

Down they moved to the beating of drums and blowing of horns, down towards the dusty plain. When they were about a mile away, Alexander ordered the trumpet to signal the advance.

Darius was positioned at the outer edge of his centre formation, seated in his royal chariot, flanked by his kinsmen, the royal Persian bodyguard – his 10,000 Immortals – with golden apples on their spear-butts, as well as Indian and Mardian warriors. On his left was the Bactrian cavalry, the Persian cavalry and infantry, then Susian and Afghan contingents. In advance of the left wing was the Scythian cavalry, 100 scythed chariots, 30 war elephants and 50 war chariots, as well as 1,000 Bactrians. To his right were troops from Syria, Mesopotamia and Medes; further along, Parthians, Sacae, Tarpurians and Hycanians, and near the centre, Albanians and Sacesinians. In advance of the right wing were a further 50 scythed chariots, the Armenian and Cappadocian cavalry and Greek mercenaries. His generals were Barsentes, Nabarzanes, Mazaeus and Bessus.

The main danger to Alexander was of being encircled by the enemy. With such overwhelming troops, the Persians would be expecting to surround his far fewer forces and annihilate them.

The battle was about to begin; the first orders shouted out to the sound of trumpets and drums. Once again, Alexander and Darius came face to face, each plainly visible to the other. Darius' scythed chariots made the first move and galloped forward into Alexander's front line.

Alexander ordered his Companions to follow him and, with their spine-chilling battle cry, "Aiaya! Aiaya! Aiaya!", went cantering to the right, in the famous oblique line which his father Philip had taught him to use to such effect, while his general, Parmenion, and the rest held back to the left.

Breaking into a furious gallop, Alexander tried to reach the far right where he knew the ground was rough and unsuitable for Darius' chariots.

His plan was to draw the Persians to his right flank, hoping that Darius' other men would try and encircle Parmenion, leaving Alexander's left flank, by which time, Alexander had calculated, he would have ridden out beyond the Persian left, thus weakening the centre of Darius's formation.

But Darius saw what he was up to and moved swiftly, sending 2,000 of his dreaded Scythian horsemen to his left. They out-galloped Alexander, and prevented him from reaching the rough ground. The Scythians began to encircle Alexander, thinking to gain an easy victory there. But they had not counted on a highly mobile flank guard of Macedonians.

700 of them charged in and diverted the Scythians from their first purpose. Behind each contingent of Alexander's cavalry were hidden a troop of foot soldiers – infantrymen. As the two sides entangled, thousands more of Alexander's men fell upon the Scythians, who found themselves outnumbered and had to retreat.

Further troops on the Persian side were sent in. In the fierce fray, the Macedonians were not only out-numbered, but less well armed. However, they fought with disciplined charge after counter charge, following Alexander's precise orders and, gradually, they forced the enemy back, breaking their formation.

The rest of Darius' left flank was forced to rush over to support them. Bowmen and infantry hurtled forward, and the scythed chariots again went into attack. But Alexander had anticipated this. He knew that chariots needed to move in a straight line to be effective, so waiting for them were his missile throwers and long-distance javelin hurlers, who cut them to pieces. A few chariots got through, their horses galloping aimlessly to be dealt with by the rear-guard.

Now it became a desperate fight; every man for himself, hurling themselves at each other, bodies entangled, swords swiping, shields clashing, horses running free as their charioteers were pulled to the ground to be trampled or slaughtered.

Desperately trying to encircle Alexander, Darius sent in his Iranian cavalry. They charged straight through, only to be met by 600 mounted sarissa-bearers, who beat them back.

Darius sent the main body of his infantry to help outflank the Macedonians, but this weakened the centre of his formation which opened up, exposing the Great King himself.

Seizing the moment, Alexander formed his Companions into a tight wedge, their thrusting sarissas held to the fore like a vast cage. With deadly purpose, they changed direction and plunged back to the weakened Persian centre, followed by spearmen, shield bearers and foot-companions.

Nearer and nearer they charged, nearer and nearer to the Great King. They came so close to Darius, that Alexander flung his spear at him and just missed, killing Darius' charioteer instead. But Alexander had aimed at the weakest point – the king himself.

Meanwhile, on Alexander's left flank, Parmenion was in trouble. Unable to join up with the right flank, he and his men had to fight it out. The Persian general, Mazaeus, sent in a charge to try and break their flank with 3,000 horsemen, but they were undisciplined, and lacked clear instructions. They charged wildly, straight into the baggage camp, landing up behind the enemy lines, where Alexander's grooms and reservists surrounded them and cut them down.

Perhaps their goal had been to rescue Darius' queen and family. Some of them found the tent in which the Persian Queen Mother, Sisygambis, and the family were being held. But when they burst in to free her, she didn't move. Not a word fell from her lips; neither her colour nor her expression changed, as she sat immobile. Uncertain whether she wanted to stay or be rescued, they fled.

Back in the fray, Alexander's men were struggling in the centre. He was desperately exposed. His outnumbered forces were having difficulty keeping their line solid. Sixty of his Companions were wounded, including Hephaistion.

Suddenly, seeing a gap among the sarissas, jubilant Indian and Persians poured through but, rather than wiping out the disarrayed Macedonians, they too aimed for the baggage tents, perhaps also wanting to rescue the Persian queen. Instead they were set upon and routed.

In the swirling dust, among the howlings of wounded elephants and horses with corpses piling up, and the screams of the dying, Darius retreated. Leaping from his chariot on to a waiting horse, as at Issus, he fled the field.

Alexander and a group of his horsemen galloped after him, but though they rode hard all the way to the Royal Road, Darius evaded them yet again.

Night fell, Alexander's horses were exhausted. He turned back empty-handed. He was still hailed as King of Asia — but he knew that until he had actually captured Darius, he couldn't call himself that.

By the time he returned to the battlefield, the battle was over. More than 3,000 of his men were dead, and the Persian army — what was left of

it — was in full retreat, leaving — how many dead? Was it 40,000, 90,000 or 300,000? Whatever the exact numbers, the battlefield was full of the dead and dying from both sides.

Alexander's victory at Gaugamela confirmed his military genius and ensured his reputation would live on through the ages to inspire Romans like Julius Caesar, and even Napoleon over a thousand years later.

Myths about Alexander were already circulating: to the Greeks, Macedonians, Egyptians and Babylonians, he was heroic and godlike; he was Ammon, Gilgamesh and Heracles.

But for the Persians and their allies, he was bloodthirsty and demonic. "Watch out, or Alexander will get you," Persian mothers told their children.

ALEXANDER THE DEMON

Alexander, who goes round pretending to be a god, is really a demon. No one knows his terrible secret except his own faithful barber — and why? Because, my little ones, hidden beneath his dark curly locks, he has two devil's horns.

One day, his barber died. Alexander knew he must get another, but how could he force him to keep the secret?

When the new barber came before him, Alexander looked at him with a terrifying gaze. "When you cut my hair," he told him in a dark, sinister

voice, "you will learn my secret. But I warn you, if you tell a single soul of what you find, I will kill you."

Sure enough, when the barber cut Alexander's hair, he saw the two horns sprouting above his ears on either side. He shook with terror and awe and amazement. What he had seen was so extraordinary, he longed to shout it out to the world. But he knew he couldn't.

But as the days and weeks and months went by, the barber knew he must tell somebody — just somebody, or he would burst.

When his work was done, he went home. "I have a secret..." He wanted to tell his wife, but clamped his mouth shut and fled away. He wandered through the town, greeting his friends and drinking palm wine with them. "I have a secret..." He wanted to tell them, but couldn't, and rushed away biting his lip.

At last he reached the open desert, where only the wind blew and the sands murmured, and there he came to an open well. He bent over the edge of the well — and far down below saw his own reflection staring wildly back up at him. "I have a secret, he screamed down the well. I have a secret, an amazing secret — but you must promise not to tell. Promise."

"Promise ... promise ... promise..."came back the echo.

"Alexander has horns!"

"Alexander has horns ... Alexander has horns ... Alexander has horns..."

At last he had told someone, and full of exultation and relief, the barber went back to his job.

But some months later, a shepherd herding his goats out in the desert paused for a rest and a drink, and noticed a single long reed growing

out of the well. "Why, that will make me a perfect pipe," he cried, and, plucking the reed, he got out his knife and shaped a mouthpiece and cut several holes for his fingers.

Then he blew, to see what kind of music he could play. But instead of music, the pipe rang out, "Alexander has horns! Alexander has horns!"

He went racing back into town. "Listen, listen!" he cried. "Listen to what I can play on my pipe."

People gathered round to hear, and the shepherd blew his reed pipe. "Alexander has horns, Alexander has horns!" it trilled.

And so the secret was out, and everyone knew that Alexander was a devil.

CHAPTER TWELVE

BABYLON

Behold Alexander, Iskander, Ishkander, Iskindar or Skander; riding into Babylon!

What an extraordinary moment it was for the people of Babylon, when Alexander entered as a conquering hero. It was 2 October, and the city's leaders and priests rode out to meet him with rich gifts. The streets were strewn with flowers, tossed beneath his chariot wheels. Darius had fled into the region of Medea, but his general, Mazaeus, who had escaped from Gaugamela, wisely surrendered to Alexander, who then made him governor of the city. But Darius' other general, Bessus, had not surrendered. Instead, he fled into the hills with troops and turned traitor to Darius. He proclaimed himself king – saying Darius had brought shame on the empire by his flight. Alexander decided to deal with him later.

For now, he marvelled at Babylon, for Babylon was the cradle of a civilization even older than that of the Greeks and Egyptians. This was

the fabulous land of the magi, seers and soothsayers; of the god Tammuz of the Abyss, and the Queen of Heaven, Ishtar. A spirit world of hostile demons, nimble as gazelles, with wings like eagles, watchful as serpents, who drank blood and devoured corpses. It was the land of the kings: Cyrus, Nebuchadnezzar and Belshazzar; of immense temples, palaces and treasures and the great Hanging Gardens.

Nebuchadnezzar II had created a vast and fabulous empire which stretched from Mesopotamia to Egypt, Palestine and the shores of the Aegean. The city of Babylon was already ancient, dating back 23 centuries BC. It had risen and fallen, but under Nebuchadnezzar II, had risen again to become the most fabulous and wealthy city in the known world. He had built the Hanging Gardens of Babylon, to help his Medean wife overcome her homesickness for the mountain scenery, of her own country. They were known as one of the Seven Wonders of the World.

He also built the Temple of Bel Marduk with its extraordinary ziggurat, seven storeys high, which later became known as the Tower of Babel. Always remembering his father's advice, Alexander paid his respects at the local temples, and offered up a sacrifice to Bel Marduk. He prayed:

I will praise the Lord of Wisdom,
Marduk, the reasonable god,
Who, like the storm of a cyclone,
Envelops everything with his wrath,
But whose breath then becomes beneficent

Like the morning zephyr!
At first his anger and rage are catastrophic,
But after, he has a change of heart.
His soul revives.

Bel Marduk was an agricultural deity, who made the plants grow and the wheat ripen. After the creation of the universe by the god of all, Ahura Mazda, it was Bel Marduk who killed the evil demon Tiamut, the goddess of chaos, and from her body, he created the earth; the mountains, seas and land below and the vault of heaven above for the moon and stars. The rivers Tigris and Euphrates flowed from her eyes, and it was between them that the city of Babylon was built and became his chosen city.

Alexander had never seen a city as huge and rich and extraordinary as Babylon, with its vast outer wall, its boulevards, tall houses and palaces.

Its opulence was almost unimaginable anywhere else in the world. He encountered its religions and philosophies, its history and culture. If Egypt would always be his spiritual home, Babylon would be his capital. "One day, this is where I will have my seat of power," declared Alexander. "Babylon will be the centre of my empire."

Amazing stories dazzled Alexander and his armies; stories about King Nebuchadnezzar, King Belshazzar, and of Daniel the Judean, the Master of Magicians, a visionary and an interpreter of dreams, who lived 300 years before Alexander was born.

BELSHAZZAR'S FEAST

After Nebuchadnezzar died, Belshazzar ruled over the empire. But like so many powerful rulers, he too became corrupt, and so did the city of Babylon.

One day, Belshazzar held a great feast and invited a thousand lords and their ladies. The wine ran freely. Belshazzar drank before them all. He brought out all the golden and silver vessels which Nebuchadnezzar had previously looted from the House of God in the temple in Jerusalem, when he had sacked the city. To the horror of the priests of the temple, Belshazzar exhorted all the princes and counsellors, their wives and concubines, to drink wine from these sacred vessels. They drank the wine and praised the heathen gods of gold, silver, brass, iron, wood and stone.

Suddenly a mysterious hand appeared. Fingers from a man's hand began to write strange words across the wall of the palace. The king saw the hand and was so terrified that the joints of his loins loosened and his knees knocked together. The king called out loud to bring in all the soothsayers, astrologers, those mystics of the Chaldeans, and all the wise men of Babylon. "Whoever can read these words and tell me what they mean, shall be clothed with scarlet and have a chain of gold about his neck, and will become third ruler in the kingdom."

From all over the city came the wise men, but not one of them could

read the strange words. The king became even more afraid, and his courtiers were amazed at how his face and demeanour changed.

Then his queen came into the chamber and said, "O King, live for ever. Let not thy thoughts trouble thee, nor let thy countenance be changed. There is a man in thy kingdom, who was known to thy father for being possessed of the holy spirit; full of light, understanding and wisdom, and whom thy father made master of all magicians, astrologers, Chaldeans and soothsayers. This man, who is such an excellent spirit has the knowledge and understanding for interpreting dreams, explaining dilemmas and dissolving doubts. His name is Daniel. Let him be called and he will surely be able to interpret these words."

So the king called forth Daniel – the same Daniel who was born of the line of Jews, who Nebuchadnezzar had enslaved, and brought into Babylon out of Jewry; the same Daniel who entered the lion's den – and he said to him, "I have heard that you are filled with the spirit of God; of light and understanding and excellent wisdom. None of my wise men and astrologers can read these words. If you can read them and tell me what they mean, then, as I have promised, you shall be clothed in scarlet, have a gold chain around your neck and be third ruler of the kingdom."

Daniel said, "I don't want your gifts. Give them to someone else. But I will read the writing on the wall."

The words were Mene, Tekel, Peres.

First, Daniel reminded Belshazzar how Nebuchadnezzar had displeased God, and had become a wild beast, who ate grass, with dew on his body, hair like feathers and nails like claws. "You too, Belshazzar, you have not humbled your heart, but you have set yourself against the Lord of Heaven.

You have taken his gold and silver vessels from the temple, and allowed the lords, their wives, concubines and ladies to drink wine from them. You have praised the gods of gold, silver, brass, wood, iron and stone which see not, hear not, know not. You have not glorified the god who gave you breath." Then he read out the words.

Mene – God hath numbered thy kingdom and finished it.

Tekel – thou art weighed in the balance and found wanting.

Peres – thy kingdom is divided and given to the Medes and Persians.

Although Daniel's words terrified him, Baelshazzar kept his promise and insisted that Daniel be clothed in scarlet, with a gold chain round his neck, and made him third ruler of the kingdom.

But Cyrus and his Persian armies were already at the gate and, in the night, Belshazzar was slain.

CHAPTER THIRTEEN

ON THE PERSIAN THRONE

This happened 300 years before Alexander came to Babylon with his armies. He was amazed at the civilization he found — older even than the Greeks — where people had written in a script called cuneiform on tablets of clay. Written down were their great stories like the epic of Gilgamesh and his beloved friend, Enkidu; stories which were sometimes told as if they were about Alexander instead of Gilgamesh; as if it was Alexander who searched for the Water of Life to save his beloved Hephaistion; Alexander who was confronted by the demon, Musas, who tried to stop him marching through the mountain; Alexander, who finally drank the Water of Life, and came out of the well, strengthened, nourished, and his flesh blue — the colour of supernatural beings such as they were in India.

But listen to the real story, or what is left of it. The story was found etched onto tablets of clay thousands of years old — so ancient that many tablets are missing and there are gaps which only the imagination can fill.

GILGAMESH, THE WARRIOR WHO DIDN'T WANT TO DIE

A baby boy was flung from the battlements of a citadel; no one knows why.

As he hurtled to the ground, an eagle swooped down, caught the infant in his talons and flew away with it. The eagle carried the child to a wondrous palace garden in the kingdom of Uruk.

He was found by the gardener and taken into the palace where, like Moses, he was adopted into the royal household and brought up as a prince called Gilgamesh.

Gilgamesh became a fearful ruler of Uruk. It had been a vast city, of great wealth, with fortifications, gardens and wonderful temples. The goddess they most venerated was Ishtar, the Queen of Heaven.

But the city of Uruk had a terrible enemy, King Humbaba, of the Great Cedar Forest, ruler of the kingdom of Elam. For years now, the Elamites had besieged Uruk, bringing famine, disease and destitution to the city. It was said that the gods had turned to flies and the winged bulls had become like mice. The people crawled on all fours and ate grass like wild beasts, and their moaning cries could be heard from afar. Although they prayed in the temple, even Ishtar seemed unable to help.

At last, the earth goddess Aruru heard their cries and prayers. She

decided to create a warrior who would save them. She dipped her hands in water and with the earth formed a giant warrior out of clay. He was named Ea-Bani which meant "Ea is my creator."

The people of Uruk got to hear of Ea-Bani, the one who might be their saviour if he could be tamed.

He was a strange man-beast, eating grass with the gazelles and drinking water with the wild animals; whose body was wet with the dew of heaven, whose hair was like eagle feathers and whose nails were like bird's claws. A hunter was sent out to find him. He took a beautiful woman with him to entice Ea-Bani out of the wild and bring him into the city. When they found Ea-Bani, the beautiful woman told him about the city of Uruk, with its marvellous temples to Ishtar, Bel and the sun god, Shamash. She also told him of the ruler, Gilgamesh, whose strength in combat was supreme.

Ea-Bani realized how lonely he was. He listened to the hunter and the beautiful woman, and heard all their stories about the city and the lives of men. He was also curious to see if he could fight Gilgamesh in single combat. So he consented to return with her and the hunter to Uruk.

But Ea-Bani was warned that his role was to be Gilgamesh's protector, and he must never allow him to be defeated in combat. So while the two men rough and tumbled and hurled themselves round the city, they ended their fight like competing brothers, and became the closest of friends, and each would fight to the death to protect each other. Now that Ea-Bani lived like a man, Gilgamesh named him Enkidu, and their love for each other was unparalleled.

The two heroes set off for the Great Cedar Forest to fight King Humbaba and the Elamites. Their journey was long, and took them through treacherous vales and high mountains until they finally came face to face with Humbaba, and, after a long, bloody fight defeated him.

Gilgamesh and Enkidu returned to their kingdom, Uruk, which then become happy and prosperous. Gilgamesh was welcomed as a hero; people adored and admired him, and when he stood in his splendid robes of state with a dazzling crown upon his head, he looked like a god himself.

But Gilgamesh was fated. The goddess Ishtar, Queen of Heaven, fell in love with him. She came to him and said, "O Gilgamesh, come with me and be my husband and I will give you a chariot made of gold, with wheels encrusted with gems and lapis lazuli, and it will be pulled by the finest of white horses. If you will be my husband, you shall dwell among the fragrant cedars and every king, prince and ruler will bow before you and kiss your feet."

Some might think this was the most wonderful thing that could happen, but it was not. Gilgamesh knew that though she was Queen of Heaven her love was not to be trusted, and he said, "Why should I believe that you would be faithful to me if I were your husband? Look what happened to your other loves: you loved Tammuz, who still weeps because of you; you loved the Alla Bird, then broke its wings; you loved the lion, then snared him; you loved the horse, then harnessed him; you loved a shepherd, who even sacrificed his goat kids to you, but you turned him into a jackal to be driven away by his own shepherd boy, and torn to pieces by the dogs; you loved the Gardener of Anu, but despite his offerings and devotion to you, you struck him so that he never

moved again. What fate would befall me, if I became your husband?"

Ishtar was furious with this rejection. She sent a monstrous bull to kill Gilgamesh. But Gilgamesh and Enkidu fought and slew the dreadful creature. When Ishtar cursed Gilgamesh, Enkidu threatened to kill her as he had killed the bull, so she cursed him too.

Soon the curse began to take effect. Gilgamesh's beloved Enkidu was afflicted by a terrible disease. Day by day, he worsened, and every night he was beset with terrible dreams. "I have seen what death is," he cried.

"What is it like down there in the Land of the Dead?"

Enkidu replied, "I don't like to tell you. It will only make you dread death all the more."

Gilgamesh insisted. "Tell me, tell me, so that I can sit and weep with you."

So Enkidu told him of a place where the ill doers were punished, where the young were like the old, where the worm devoured everything, and dust covered everything; where the state of the warrior who had been given a burial was better than the warrior who had not, and who had no one to lament over him; where even kings squatted in the darkness with dirt for food and clay for drink.

"I will pray to the gods and beg them to show you mercy," wept Gilgamesh.

But Enkidu replied, "My fate is settled. There is nothing you can do," and he slowly died.

Gilgamesh was heartbroken. "What is this sleep which has come over you?" he wept. "You have turned dark and do not hear me!" He bent over his friend looking for signs of life, but Enkidu's eyes did not move and

when he pressed his ear to Enkidu's heart, it no longer beat. Gilgamesh covered his friend's face like a bride.

With terrible lamenatations, Gilgamesh cut off his hair, scattering his curls upon the ground. He took off all his fine ornaments and clothes and called upon all, from Uruk as far as the Great Cedar Forest, to mourn his friend.

"My beloved friend is dead. His spirit is a prisoner of the Spirits of Death in the Underworld? Oh Enkidu!" wept Gilgamesh. "Now you will never draw your bow, nor shout the battle cry, nor embrace the woman you love, nor kiss your beloved child, nor will you be able to fight with those that hate you."

Then something terrible happened to Gilgamesh. He became afraid, for he too was afflicted with a disease. Despite all his heroism and famous deeds in battle, faced with the loss of his friend, the reality of death and how absolute it was, how inevitable and irretrievable it was, struck him to the core. He was afraid of death. He wept and cried out to the gods, "Oh, let me not die like Enkidu, for death is fearful!" Now his one thought was to find a way to avoid death himself.

Gilgamesh set off alone on his quest. He had heard of an island which was to be found in the Ocean of Death, and where his ancient ancestor Utnapishtim lived. Utnapishtim had succeeded in defying death and could live for ever. Perhaps his ancestor could tell him where to find the Water of Life and where he could pluck the Plant of Life.

The journey was full of perils and hardship: Gilgamesh fought lions and other wild beasts; he descended into sunless chasms, crossed rocky ranges, and scaled mountains until he came to the vast mountain peak of

Mount Mashu, whose foundations were in Aralu, the Nether World, but whose peak rose as high as heaven.

A long tunnel ran through this mountain, which Gilgamesh knew would bring him to the shores of the Ocean of Death. He searched the sides of the mountain to gain entry and came to a door. But barely had he found the door when he fainted with horror at the sight of two fearsome creatures which guarded the entrance into the mountain — two gigantic scorpions, with vast scaly bodies, burning tails, and heads which reached into the clouds. When Gilgamesh came to his senses, he found the two monsters had not harmed him at all, but gazed over him with sympathetic eyes.

"What brings you to this lost and dreadful place?" they asked.

Gilgamesh told them how he was searching for his ancestor, Utnapishtim.

"The dangers are great," warned the giant scorpions. "Turn back, turn back."

If Gilgamesh was afraid of death, he wasn't afraid of dangers. "I will face whatever perils cross my path," he said. So the scorpions opened the door and he crossed the threshold into the start of the tunnel. The door slammed behind him, leaving him in impenetrable darkness. For twelve miles he groped his way blindly along the passage until at last, 24 hours later, he glimpsed a ray of light. Filled with joy and renewed energy, he ran towards it.

It was like running into paradise. Bursting out into glorious sunshine, he found himself in a beautiful garden of flowers, shrubs, bushes and trees of every kind. But most wondrous of all, in the middle of the garden, was

an amazing tree on whose branches hung clusters of jewels and leaves of lapis lazuli. Although the temptation was almost unbearable, Gilgamesh managed to tear himself away from the beautiful garden, and hurried on until he came to the shore of the Ocean of Death.

This country by the sea was ruled by a sea lady called Siduri. When he told her he wanted to sail across the sea, she tried to persuade him to turn back. "Accept your portion in life and what God has given you. Besides, no one but the god Shamash has ever crossed these billows of death. The way is full of peril."

But though Gilgamesh was now full of disease and sorely stricken, he would not be put off and accept his fate. He cried, "I must cross the Ocean of Death and find my ancestor, Utnapishtim."

At last the lady told him of a boatman called Arad Ea, who once served Utnapishtim, and who might help him. Gilgamesh went in search of him and, finally, after much pleading, persuaded Arad Ea to ferry him across the water.

They endured terrible experiences crossing the Ocean of Death, but finally, they arrived, exhausted, at the Island of the Blessed on which dwelt Gilgamesh's ancestor, Utnapishtim, and his wife.

But now, Gilgamesh's strength was completely spent, and he hadn't the energy to go ashore. So he just sat there in the boat, too ill to move. However, Utnapishtim had seen the boat approaching and, marvelling that anyone could have crossed the Ocean of Death, came down to the shore.

"What brings you to my dreadful shore?" Utnapishtim asked Gilgamesh.

Gilgamesh told him of his troubles and sufferings; how all he longed to

do was escape the curse of his disease by bathing in the Water of Life, and to take back the Plant of Life. "How is it that you, O revered ancestor, have eternal life and no one else? What must I do to get it too, for death hovers round me now, waiting to snatch away my soul?"

Then Utnapishtim told him how God had warned him that he was going to send a mighty flood. That he had obeyed God's instructions and built an ark, and taken onboard the lion, the mule, the raven and the dove, and all living things, so that they may flourish once more in a new land. For this favour, God had rewarded him with everlasting life.

Utnapishtim tried to reason with Gilgamesh. "All men must die," he reminded him. "They build houses, seal contracts with each other, quarrel with each other, sow seeds, reap crops – and continue in this way till death comes. Nor does any man know the hour of his death. Only the God of Destiny who has measured out the span of life for each man – only he knows the secret and will never tell."

But Gilgamesh refused to give up and said he wanted to receive the same blessings as his ancestor. So Utnapishtim relented. He told Gilgamesh to sit for six days and seven nights as one in meditation.

Gilgamesh was enveloped by a deep sleep. While he slept, Utnapishtim and his wife circled the young man and took pity on him. They prepared magic food and gave it to him while he slept so that when, on the seventh day, Utnapishtim touched Gilgamesh and woke him, the young warrior was amazed to feel full of life and energy. Now he could continue his journey.

Utnapishtim instructed the boatman to take Gilgamesh to a fountain of healing water. Here, after bathing in the waters, his diseased skin fell

away and he was cured. All he needed now before returning home was the Plant of Life. Then the boatman took him to an island where this magic plant grew. Gilgamesh plucked it and rejoiced and was immediately eager to return to the city of Uruk.

Gilgamesh bade farewell to Utnapishtim, and was rowed back across the ocean to begin the return journey. But the journey back was no less perilous than coming.

One day, Gilgamesh stopped at a well to drink, laying down the Plant of Life on the ground. While he sated his thirst, a snake, smelling the plant's beautiful fragrance, slithered forward and stole it. Gilgamesh was terror-sricken. "Oh Arad Ea! All my suffering has been for nothing!"

With heavy heart, he continued on his way until he reached the walls of Uruk. But though his eyes gazed upon the ramparts gleaming in the sun of this incomparable city: though he climbed the stone steps to the great temple of Ishtar, and gazed around the palm trees, gardens, orchards and marketplaces, Gilgamesh...

And so the story dwindles away. If Alexander hoped to hear a happy ending, I cannot give it. It seems there is no happy ending — if happiness means succeeding in the quest for everlasting life. Not even Alexander can hope for that.

But wherever he went, he heard this story — or something like it; stories of Heracles, or Prince Rama of India in the Ramayan, all give the same message, that a hero must be comforted by the words of wisdom; live his best, love his loved ones, rejoice in food and bathing and clean clothes;

be inspired by music and poetry and all the good things in life; not ask to control the time of his death, for that is in the hands of the gods and, above all, fear God and keep his commandments. This is what was written on those tablets of clay.

Weep now, Alexander! Even Hephaistion must die one day, and the sorrow you feel will be as great as that of Gilgamesh for Enkidu, and Achilles for Patroclus.

Despite the wonders of Babylon, Alexander only stayed there for five weeks. He had to keep pressing on until he had defeated Darius, for conquering Babylon was not conquering Asia.

THE SEAT OF
KINGS

Having appropriated the treasures and established rule under Mazaeus, he was on the road again heading for the ancient palace in Susa.

Susa was the centre of administration for the Persian empire, and the heart of its power. He might have expected heavy resistance, but, perhaps because Darius had disgraced himself by running away, there was very little.

Alexander entered the great palace of Susa and sat on the golden throne of kings. One of his followers burst into tears to see a Greek ruler sitting on the Persian throne at last.

However, it could have been an embarrassing moment for Alexander. Although he was famous for his godlike beauty, he was not tall. This throne had been designed for Darius, who was over six feet, and when Alexander sat down on it, his feet didn't touch the ground, but dangled like a child's.

Disconcerted, he swung his legs on to a small table, causing one of

Darius' household to weep and wail at the lack of respect. Attendants at the scene noticed Alexander hesitate — one part of him didn't wish to humiliate the Persians, or perform an ignorant act of discourtesy, but he kept his feet on the table, to save face and demonstrate his absolute power.

Alexander stayed in Susa just long enough to make sure it was under his control — albeit under the command of a Persian. This was his way — to allow those who surrendered to him to worship their own gods and be ruled by one of themselves, though under overall Greek control.

He left Darius' mother, Queen Sisygambis, his wife and children safely in Susa, and continued on his way. The next stop was in the very heart of Persia, Persepolis.

CHAPTER 14

PERSEPOLIS

It wasn't an easy march. Alexander's army was now up against stiff local resistance.

They reached a sheer wall of rock known as the Gates of Persia. It was approached by a narrow gorge; a perfect place for an ambush.

In one of the few setbacks of Alexander's campaign, a huge contingent of Persians lay in wait, desperate to prevent him reaching Persepolis. They were hidden high up among the rocks and, as Alexander's troops approached, they hurled huge rocks and boulders down on top of them, and flung stones from catapults. Many of his men were killed and wounded, and they were forced to retreat – a reverse Alexander was not used to. It only made him more determined to succeed whatever the cost.

A local shepherd came forward, a man who was part Lycian, part Persian. Perhaps he had a grievance against the Persians, but he offered to help Alexander. He knew of a rough secret track which went round the gorge. It was steep and dangerous, but it led to the Persian camp.

Alexander cunningly ordered part of his army to make camp, so that the Persians would see the fires of about 4,000 men, burning through the night, and would think themselves safe. Meanwhile, with three days' supply of food, he took the majority of his men and mules and followed the shepherd through the freezing darkness, until they reached the high plateau where he found the Persians' camp.

He slaughtered them without mercy.

Winter was approaching; the winter of 331 BC. It was cold, and would get colder, with torrential rain and snow flurries. The near disastrous engagement at the Gates of Persia had left Alexander shaken, and his men uncertain. They needed rewards to compensate them for the immense rigours and privation of their campaigns.

They had crossed the River Araxes and reached a broad plain surrounded by hills. They were now in the heart of Persia on the road to Persepolis, the capital palace city of the Persian kings.

The Greeks had talked of Persepolis for generations. They knew its meaning and significance. This was the city most hated by the Greeks for what it represented: the power of the first Persian King Darius, and his son Xerxes, who had poured into Greece with his armies. The Greeks still shuddered with the humiliating memory, passed down from generation to generation, of how, in 480 BC the Persian king, Xerxes, actually reached Athens and burned down the temples of the Acropolis. Now it was the turn of the Greeks. They were about to hold Persepolis in their hands. What a glorious revenge!

As its tall towers and pillars glimmered into sight, hundreds of men suddenly appeared before them on the road, waving branches to show they came in peace. Alexander brought his horse to a standstill; he was filled with shock and pity, for most of the men were old and had been mutilated in some way: noses and ears cut off, or hands and legs. It brought tears to his eyes.

They told him they were Greek artists and craftsmen, who had been enslaved by the Persians years before, and brought to Persepolis to work on the city palace. Their mutilations had been carefully carried out so that they could use their skills, but not run away.

Alexander was so moved, he wanted to arrange for them to be sent home immediately. But they were old and incapacitated, and the prospect of trying to integrate back into their previous lives was more than they could bear. They told him they would rather stay where they were, but they wanted his protection. Alexander therefore gave each of them 3000 drachmae, five men's robes and five women's robes, two yoke of oxen and 50 sheep, and 50 measures of corn. He also exempted them from all taxes and warned his officials that they were never to be ill-treated.

It was with added hatred that Alexander gazed at the Persian city palace before him.

It was a glorious city palace – as glorious as the Temple of Solomon. It was built over a vast area, with winding walls and fortifications, temples and towers. If the houses for the private citizens were sumptuously furnished and overflowing with opulence, it was the palace which astonished Alexander with its bronze gates, gold-plated walls, huge doors of cedar, and tall fluted columns of marble, whose plinths were carved with monstrous mythical animals. Flanking the stairways, giant reliefs depicted gods and kings and Persian life, attendants serving, noble horses pulling chariots into battle, and hunters chasing gazelles and fighting with leaping lions. There were vast staircases leading to amazing platforms and halls — including the great 100-columned hall where the king received important guests from all over the world.

All that was most magnificent in Persian culture — sculpture, architecture, and art — was here.

If Alexander was impressed by the beauty of the palace, he was more impressed by the knowledge that he was at the core of the Persian Empire; the symbol of its wealth and power; the heart of its civilization. This was the prize. With Persepolis in his hands, he would have the jewel, the very soul of Persia. For him, it was the most hateful city in Asia.

Alexander was 25 years old. His youth took over; his blood was up. He wanted revenge.

Sparing the palace, Alexander let his men loose on the city. They ripped through the streets and houses and villas and temples, killing the men, raping and enslaving the women and girls. Homes were stripped, vandalized and pillaged; the soldiers staggered out with armfuls of gold and silver, ornaments and jewellery, with purple and gold cloth, and wonderful artefacts. Consumed by greed, lust and demonic energy, they looted, smashed and destroyed till, within hours, a city which had taken generations to build was in ruins.

This was Alexander's way of repaying his men for their fortitude and loyalty, and of giving them the will to carry on the campaign — for carry on he would. By the time everything calmed down, he had already appropriated the bulk of the treasure in the palace storehouse and cleared Persepolis of all its wealth. It took 3,000 pack camels and a great number of mules to carry it all to safety. Alexander then proceeded to restore order to the city – or what was left of it. He organized a system of taxation and structure, as he had done with all the other cities, and installed a Persian governor as ruler.

Winter was now upon them, with torrential rain and sudden falls of snow – not a good season to continue campaigning, so Alexander stayed in Persepolis for four months. It was not in his nature to do nothing, so he went out in the hills, hunting, and also fitted in the conquest of the former capital, Pasagarde, another seat of Persian power, succeeding easily with the collaboration of its Persian administrators.

Not far from Pasagarde was the tomb of Cyrus the Great, who Alexander greatly admired from all he had heard about him. As king of Persia, he had conquered Babylon and the land of the Chaldeans. His goal had been to conquer the universe. Though he ruled over 200 years before Alexander was born, his fame was known throughout the ancient world.

Alexander knew that Cyrus had been famous, not just for being a conqueror, but for being a civilized and merciful man, who respected other people's religions and customs. He had formulated a Charter of Human Rights, and returned captured people to their own country. Enslaved Jews had sung, "By the rivers of Babylon, there we sat down, yea we wept when we remembered Zion" – and Cyrus had allowed them to go back to their own lands.

Alexander honoured him.

But Cyrus would have wept at what this young man did next, this youth who could alternate between behaving like a god and hero, then acting like a beast; who could plan as brilliantly as any military strategist, then suddenly be feckless and blindly destructive.

Alexander returned to Persepolis from the tomb of Cyrus. Oh, what a disastrous return. It was as if he was besotted with the wealth and power which now lay in his hands. There was much feasting, drinking and debauchery and, one night, in one senseless act, the Palace of Persepolis was burned to the ground. How could a man of Alexander's taste and refinement have allowed this?

THE BURNING OF PERSEPOLIS

There was a drunken party with flowing wine and whirling dancers. They say a beautiful dancing girl, Thais, took Alexander's hand and, as he was intoxicated, enticed him and his guests to frolic wantonly through the palace with firebrands in their hands. His general, Parmenion, begged Alexander not to destroy the palace. "After all, why burn what is yours?"

But they egged each other on, laughing and joking, thrusting their fiery brands at the silken drapes, the rich brocades, the soft furnishings and the hanging carpets. Soon the palace was ablaze. The fire spread, consuming the magnificent wooden panels and floors, which came crashing down. The glow was seen with horror for miles around.

By dawn, the glorious palace city was reduced to ash. It was an act of destruction which many would never forgive.

The burning of Persepolis should have marked the end of the Greek revenge on the Persians. But the Great King Darius was still free and was boasting that he was still king.

CHAPTER FIFTEEN

THE DEATH OF DARIUS

That dreadful winter fades away. The spring of 330 BC stirs their bones.

Darius needed friends; he needed to raise a further army, but doubt had spread among the people. They knew that Alexander was coming after Darius; Alexander, who had overpowered Babylon, Susa, Persepolis and Pasagarde, would not give up. With his supporters falling away, Darius was forced to flee Ecbatana, marching eastwards to the Caspian Gates, over the mountains of the Hindu Kush to Bactria, where he hoped to reform his power base.

However, worse was still to come for the Great King. His own generals, Barsentes and Nabarzanes plotted against him, instigated by Bessus. They planned to arrest Darius, and if Alexander caught up with them, to surrender to him and hand over their king. If, however, Alexander turned back, then they would rule and re-enforce their own powers. It was pure treason.

But Alexander was never going to turn back. Even with Persepolis

burned to the ground, he was determined not just to have Darius surrender but to prevent a new power base being built up by Bessus.

Then news came that Darius had been captured by his treacherous general. Two of Darius' loyal senior men reported Bessus' plan to Alexander, and told him where he had last camped with the prisoner king.

Alexander was galvanized into action. Leaving the women, children and other camp followers to journey at their own pace, he took a contingent of his toughest men. Carrying only their weapons, they set off along the road eastwards, riding at such breakneck speed that some of the horses died on the way.

After riding day and night for two days, they reached Bessus' camp, only to find it deserted. But they were told the stories were true. King Darius had been arrested and taken off in a covered wagon, and Bessus had declared himself ruler.

Losing no time, Alexander continued the chase. Taking those of his men who weren't too exhausted, he rode all day, ordering the rest to follow. He found a shortcut that would enable him to catch up with the king and, at last, as another night was falling, they came across straggling Persian soldiers. Some fought, many ran away.

Realizing that Alexander was upon them, Nabarzanes and Barsentes struck and assassinated their king in his wagon, then fled.

Dawn was breaking when Alexander and his men arrived at a pitiful scene. They wandered among the dead, turning the bodies over to see if Darius was among them. Strewn all around were abandoned wagons and weapons, but there was no sign of the king.

They were preparing to hurry on, following the trail, when a soldier

happened to notice an upturned cart lying in a ditch. Casually, he prodded the covering away and peered inside. There lay Darius, the Great King, shackled in gold chains; murdered by his own officers.

There was an awestruck silence. After so many conflicts and battles, after such epic struggles between the two men, even his enemies felt an overwhelming sense of tragedy to see this god-king reduced to such a pathetic and ignominious state. Alexander was so moved that he stripped off his own cloak and laid it respectfully over the dead king.

He took Darius' body back to Persepolis and there he was given a royal funeral befitting the Great King. As far as Alexander was concerned, Darius had not been defeated in battle. Bessus and his cohorts had committed regicide – an act Alexander vowed to avenge. If any of his men harboured the hope that, with the Persian king dead, Alexander would be ready to go home, they were disappointed. Bessus was raising troops in Bactria, and calling himself King. Alexander was determined to destroy him.

It was the height of summer when, in 330 BC Alexander set off again in the searing heat. Months of hard campaigning took him and his army across hostile deserts and mountainous terrain from the Iranian Plateau to Kabul; from the River Oxus to Samarkand. He traversed the land of ancient heroes: of the mythical king of Iran, Afrasiab, and of the heroes Kai Khosrow, Goodarz, Piran, Sohrab and Rostam.

Darius had been betrayed by his own followers, and Alexander too was in danger of rebellion from among his own officers.

THE SMILE THAT MEANT DEATH

Why? Was it because they were tired of war and wanted

to go home? Was it because Alexander had become bedazzled by the wealth and power he had achieved – so much so that it had gone to his head?

Or was it because, despite himself, Alexander had come to admire the Persian culture and way of life so much that it was more than the Greeks could bear?

He had taken on Persian courtly customs; wearing their dress and acquiring their manners. This enraged the Greeks both in the army and at home – for even though the troops were out in the wilds of Central Asia, there was regular communication between the army and Athens. Athens received bulletins and messages from the historians and diarists travelling with the army. Athens knew what Alexander was doing almost every inch of the way.

By now, he had fallen out with his tutor, Aristotle, who regarded any non-Greek as "barbarian". Callisthenes, Alexander's historian and fellow pupil of Aristotle, had been sending back reports which disturbed the authorities in Athens, especially Demosthenes, who loathed Alexander, believing him to show signs of behaving like an eastern despot rather than a Greek democrat. "Well what would you expect of a simpleton?" he sneered.

Many were plotting against Alexander in Athens. Closer to hand, his officers and generals were increasingly outraged by the number of Persians coming into their army, and were suspicious of how close and influential they were. Yet the rank and file of Alexander's army still adored him. He treated them like brothers and comrades in arms. He led from the front: if they were wounded, so was he; if they hungered and thirsted, so did he;

if there was a bridge to be built, or a road to be cleared, he was among them, working with his own bare hands, and if there was a wounded man to be tended, he was often there to tend him, as he had been educated in medicine and the treatment of illnesses.

In the autumn, at Drangiana, one of his oldest friends, Philotas, was accused of treason and executed. Worse still, Philotas was the son of Parmenion, his most senior and trusted general. Alexander could not believe Philotas had been part of a plot to kill him without the knowledge and approval of his father. Parmenion was in Ecbatana. Alexander sent a messenger to him with a forged letter purporting to be from Philotas. The letter said that the plot had been successful and that Alexander was dead. He told the messenger to judge from the expression on Parmenion's face whether he was guilty or innocent.

When Parmenion read the letter, he smiled. Thus was he judged and instantly assassinated.

Did Parmenion, his senior general, who had fought alongside Alexander's father, deserve such an ignominious death? Could Alexander not have shown him compassion? Remember that family loyalty was more important even than loyalty to a king. With Parmenion's son already executed, Alexander would not have been able to trust the father ever again, for the murder of a family member required the automatic necessity for another of the family to take revenge.

Alexander may have conquered the palaces of Persia, but he was still assailed by uprisings from every quarter, which he had to quell. With utter ruthlessness, he crushed any opposition from towns and villages, massacring

all the men, and enslaving the women and children. But nothing deterred him from his pursuit of Bessus. Although he came up against Sogdian and Scythian units of the Persian army, and though he was concussed, wounded and ill, Alexander still went on and on, hard on the traitor's heels. At last, in the spring of 329 BC, he caught up with him.

It had been a desperate chase: Alexander and his men had scaled the peaks and passes of the Hindu Kush, suffering incredible hardship. Bessus' scorched earth policy had destroyed the crops, bringing the army to the edge of starvation. But they kept on his trail and followed him down to the fertile plains of Bactria, where they found the Persian general had already declared himself the Great King.

Surprised that Alexander had caught up with him so quickly, Bessus abandoned Bactria and fled to the other side of the River Oxus into Sogdiana, desperately burning every boat, ferry and bridge he could find. But he reckoned without Alexander's ingenuity. Alexander ordered his men to do what the locals did – stuff ox hides with straw and float across the river.

By now, time and friends had run out for Bessus. A Sogdian nobleman called Spitamenes betrayed him, just as Besus had betrayed Darius.

Spitamenes handed Bessus over to Alexander. Bessus was humiliated and tortured in the Persian manner, which was to have his ears and nose cut off. Then he was taken back to Ecbatana, to be tried and judged by his own people at an assembly of Medes and Persians, and executed.

But this was still not the end of the road for Alexander. There were uprisings breaking out everywhere. Battles he thought he'd won had to be fought again.

Throughout the year 328 BC he fought Scythians, Bactrians and Sogdians. Alexander and his men struggled over icy mountains, starving, and eating their mules; they died, fell by the wayside, were wounded and endured all kinds of injuries while being constantly attacked by local tribes. Alexander, too, suffered from a broken fibula when it was pierced by an arrow. But still he struggled on.

This was the land of the Oxus — and from there the road led to Samarkand.

CHAPTER SIXTEEN

SAMARKAND

Nowhere are there greater stories to be found than in this ancient land, here on the banks of the Oxus; children are told of heroic deeds, great villains and past heroes. They hear of Ahriman the Evil, and Zohak, the Serpent. They hear of Zal, who was born with the white hair of an old man, and was abandoned to die by Saum, his father, because he feared that his child's white hair was an evil omen. But Zal was saved by a marvellous bird, who reared him as her own until one day, full of repentance, Saum came and reclaimed his son. This son, Zal, was to be the father of Rostam, who was then to become the father of a miraculous child, Sohrab.

Before there had even been a Persian Empire, tribes of Turks, Pehlivas, Iranians and Tartars all fought one another, creating incredible myths of tragedy and heroism.

Night after night, weary with battle, Alexander's soldiers gather round listening to the storytellers. How they stir up the blood, and restore courage and valour to Alexander's men. No story was listened to more eagerly than the sorrowful tale of Sohrab and Rostam.

SOHRAB AND ROSTAM

Rostam of Pehliva was as fine a warrior as any that Alexander knew — comparable to Heracles or Achilles. Everyone feared him.

One day, his wonderful horse, Rakhsh was stolen from him. His search led him to Samarkand. The King of Samarkand welcomed Rostam into the palace and, that night, held a great feast in his honour. There was much food, plenty of wine, and singers and dancers who performed in his honour. Finally he was led to a couch scented with musk and roses, and there he lay down and fell into a deep sleep.

It was nearly dawn, and the morning star gleamed in the sky, when into Rostam's chamber came a silent slave holding a burning lamp which exuded the sweet smell of amber. Behind the slave was a mysterious, veiled woman. She came to his bed, and he awoke, still heavy with wine and sleep.

"Who are you, and what are you doing here?" he asked.

She said, "I am Tahmineh, the daughter of the King of Samarkand. We are of the race of the leopard and the lion, yet there is no man in this city worthy of my hand. I have heard of your valour, your incredible deeds, that the earth groans beneath your feet and many warriors have

perished at your hand. No man has ever seen me unveiled, yet I have come to your chamber to tell you that I wish to be your wife. What a mighty son you and I could have, if you will accept my hand. In return, I will lead you to your horse, Rakhsh." The princess drew aside her veil to reveal a woman as fair as the moon.

Rostam thought of his wonderful horse and of the beautiful Tahmineh who could be his for the asking, and he agreed.

The marriage took place with all the rites and customs, and everyone praised Rostam and Tahmineh. Rostam embraced his bride, and took from his upper arm an onyx bracelet. "If you should give birth to a daughter, bind her hair into this bracelet, and it will shield her from all evil. But if we should have a son, let him put it on his arm and wear it as his father does. Then he will be as tall as Saum, the son of Neriman, as strong as Keriman, and with the gift of speech like my father, Zal."

The next day, as Tahmineh had promised, his steed, Rakhsh, was brought to him. Rostam was overjoyed. He saddled the horse himself, groomed its sleek body, and held its beloved head in his arms. Now he was longing to be off again. He kissed his new wife, gazed at her lovely face and caressed her hair, and told her he must go. And, so he should not be weakened by her beauty, he leaped onto his horse and galloped away.

As Rostam rode on to Zabulistan, he decided to tell no one of his marriage.

In due course, Tahmineh gave birth to a son. Straight away, he looked like his father, and was so full of smiles, that they called him Sohrab. Sohrab was a miracle. When he was only a month old, he was like a twelve-year-old; when he was five, he was already a warrior, skilled in the

arts of war. When he was ten, no one in the land was stronger than he.

One day, Sohrab came to his mother. "I am taller and stronger than any man in the city, yet I do not know who my father is. I order you to tell me!"

Tahmineh smiled. Sohrab reminded her so much of Rostam. "Don't be angry, my dear son. Be joyful, for you are of the seed of Saum and Zal and thy forefather was Neriman. Your father is Rostam the Pehliva – the like of which has never been created by God." Then she put the onyx bracelet on his arm and gave him many jewels which his father had left for his child. But Tahmineh said, "Sohrab, you must keep this a secret. Our kingdom of Turan lies under the power of the terrible Iranian, Afrasiab. Afrasiab fears your father's might and power. If he ever hears you are the son of Rostam, he will slay you.

"Mother! You should have told me before. Everyone has heard of Rostam the Pehliva. I will lead an army of Turks against the Iranians and overthrow Afrasiab. Then I shall give Father, the Crown of Kaianides and you will be Queen of Iran and Turan. Everyone will be united! O Mother, I pant with longing to ride into battle and find my father."

Afrasiab had always been afraid that Rostam, the Pehliva, might one day challenge his authority and take Iran for himself. When he heard that a Turkish army led by a mighty young warrior called Sohrab, was planning to attack Iran, he devised a secret plan. "If Rostam can be persuaded to fight on our side, and if he and this young Turk Sohrab can be tricked into combat, perhaps Sohrab will kill Rostam. I can then slay Sohrab, thus disposing of both!"

But Rostam had quarrelled with the Iranians and, at first, refused to fight. Afrasiab sent messengers to plead with him. They told him about Sohrab, the young Turk who was conquering everyone in his path. "Do not let Iran suffer. Iran has done no wrong, and does not deserve to perish at the hands of an upstart. Do not let Iran say that Rostam fled in the face of the enemy; that you were afraid to fight a beardless boy."

The cymbals clashed and the war cries sounded. Sohrab led his army into Iran slaughtering and leaving a fiery path of destruction in his wake. The Iranians were terrified. "Who can stand against this Turk?" they wailed. "Call for Rostam, the Pehliva! Unto Rostam alone must we Iranians look for help in this danger!"

At last Rostam agreed to return to the palace with them and pledged to fight for Iran.

The grey mist of dawn hung over the River Oxus. The armies were hushed with sleep, waiting for the morning when battle would begin. Only Sohrab, in the Tartar camp, had been sleepless. Finally he rose before the sun was up and put on his armour. Taking a captive Iranian called Hujir, he went to a peak overlooking the Iranian camp. Sohrab wanted to know if Rostam was among them. Hujir would recognize him.

"If you answer my questions truthfully," he told Hujir, "I will set you free."

They looked upon the tents spread below. One was of gold brocade, adorned with the skins of leopards, and guarded by 100 war elephants. Within its entrance was a throne of turquoise, and overhead floated a standard of violet, with a moon and a sun embroidered at its centre. "Whose tent is that?" he asked.

"It belongs to Kai Kavoos," replied Hujir.

Above another tent floated a standard with an elephant. "This is the tent of Tus, son of Nuder," said Hujir.

"And that one?" Sohrab pointed to a tent with a golden flag of gold, whose ensign was a lion, around which stood eighty mighty warriors.

"That belongs to Gudarz the brave, and the warriors are his sons, all sprung from his loins."

Then he saw a tent of green. Before its doors was the flag of Kawah. Seated on its throne was a warrior of the Pehliva tribe, so much taller than the rest that his head seemed to reach the stars. Beside him stood a horse as tall as he and as powerful. A fluttering standard depicted a lion and a writhing dragon.

"Whose tent is that?"

Hujir hesitated. He didn't want to betray Rostam. "His name is not known to me, though I believe he is some warrior come from far Cathay to fight for the Shah," he replied.

Sohrab was puzzled. He was desperate to identify Rostam's tent. Why did Hujir know everyone's tent, except the green one? He asked again and again, "To whom does the green tent belong – is it Rostam's?"

"No, no!" stammered Hujir. "Rostam is in Zabulistan for the feast of the roses."

But Sohrab couldn't believe that the Iranians would fight without Rostam. He turned on Hujir. "If you don't tell me which is Rostam's tent, I'll kill you."

Hujir knew that if he betrayed the tent, he would be killed by the Iranians, and if he didn't he would be killed by Sohrab. "Why seek Rostam now?" he asked, fatalistically. "You'll know him soon . He will soon strike thee dumb and quell thy pride of youth. I will not show him to thee."

Furiously, Sohrab struck off the man's head, and bellowed, "Where is the man who will do battle with me?" He hoped to lure Rostam from his tent.

His thunderous voice made the Iranians turn pale. They all knew that only Rostam's sword could cause the sun to weep. They swept over to the green tent and called upon him.

"Rostam, come out! Only you can fight this young lion!" They gathered round him and buckled on his armour and threw a leopard skin around his shoulders.

Just as Afrasiab had hoped, Rostam went down onto the plain that lay between the two camps to where Sohrab waited.

When Rostam saw the wondrous boy, so like the son he wished he had, the old warrior cried, "O young man. The air is soft and warm, but the ground is cold. I do not wish to take your life. If we fight, you will surely fall beneath my hands, for none have withstood my strength — neither men nor demons nor dragons. Leave the ranks of those Tartars of Turan. Join me instead."

"O hero!" replied Sohrab. "I seek one man, and ask only one question. What is your name? Are you Rostam, son of Zal, son of Saum, son of Neriman."

But Rostam did not tell him the truth. He wanted to persuade him to give up, not fight. "I am not Rostam," shouted. "Rostam is a Pehliva not an Iranian. I am just a slave, without crown or throne. Give up now, or soon your bones will whiten along the banks of the Oxus."

Sohrab was full of sorrow. This was not his father. His hopes, which had risen so high, were shattered, and the day which had seemed so bright, darkened at these words.

"Do you think you can frighten me?" Sohrab cried angrily. "I am no girl to be made pale by your words," and, lifting his spear to the shoulder, he hurled it at Rostam's feet and challenged him.

The two heroes flew at each other; they fought till their spears splintered, they hacked till their swords bent, they clawed at each other with their bare hands till their mail was torn from their bodies and sweat and blood ran into the sand. When they fell apart, each too exhausted to move, Rostam knew he had never fought with such a warrior. They fought till the sun darkened over their heads, and a moaning wind swept the sand around them like a shroud. With bloodshot eyes and heaving chests, they crashed together, pulling each other off their horses and rolling on the ground. Then, with one last desperate lunge, Sohrab hurled himself at Rostam and broke his sword at the hilt.

Rostam opened his mouth and bellowed into the air "Rostam!"

Sohrab heard the name and hesitated.

Rostam flung his final spear.

Sohrab was struck. He dropped his shield before the advancing giant. He staggered back, sinking to the ground, mortally wounded. It was the end. "All I wanted was to find my father," he gasped. "I tell you, even if you became a fish and swam in the deepest water, even if you became a star, and tried to hide in the heavens, heed me well, when my father learns of my death, he will come after you. My father, Rostam, will be told that I, Sohrab, his son, perished seeking for him."

Horror-struck, Rostam fell to the ground next to the dying boy. "Do you have any proof? Do you carry any token of Rostam about you? I must know if what you say is true, for I am Rostam the Pehliva."

"Why didn't you tell me your name?" wept Sohrab. "I tried to recognize you. Now it's too late. Open my armour, and you will find a jewel upon my arm — an onyx — given to me by my father so that he should know me."

Rostam opened the young boy's armour. There on his arm was the onyx. He howled with grief and tore his clothes. Tears of penitence flowed like a river from his eyes. But Sohrab sighed with his dying breath, "Weep not, my father. It is all in vain. There is no remedy. Doubtless it was written that this should be so. All I beg is that the Iranians take not vengeance on the men of Turan. If I came like the thunder, now am I vanished like the wind. Pray that we meet again in paradise."

Rostam set up such a wailing as the earth had never heard before. "I that am old have killed my son. I that am strong have uprooted this mighty boy. I have torn the heart of my child. I have laid low the head of Pehliva."

Then he made a great fire and flung upon it his tent, his trappings, his leopard skin and armour and all his weapons.

Sohrab's body was swathed in rich cloth of gold brocade encrusted with many jewels, and made ready to return to Zabulistan. Nobles marched before the bier, beating their chests with their fists, their heads covered in ashes and their garments torn with grief. The drums of the war elephants were broken and the cymbals smashed. All the tails of the horses were shorn to the root, and everywhere were the signs of mourning.

News spread to Samarkand, that Sohrab was dead. When Tahmineh heard, she wept bitterly, rolling on the ground in agony and covering her head with earth. When his clothes and horse were brought to her, she kissed them as if he still wore them; she caressed his horse and cut off its tail. She gave all his jewels to the poor. Finally, Tahmineh set fire to the house of Sohrab, and after a year of grief, the breath went out of her body and her spirit fled in search of her son, Sohrab.

"O warriors of Alexander!" the storytellers sing. "Give ear to the story of Sohrab and Rostam — a tale as sorrowful as any you may hear."

CHAPTER SEVENTEEN

IN THE FOOTSTEPS OF DIONYSUS

It is the spring of 328 BC and Bessus is vanquished. Alexander is the unchallenged King of Kings, and still he doesn't turn back. Ahead, over the Hindu Kush is India. As Alexander makes his way towards India, he walks in the footsteps of Dionysus.

Thousands of years before, Dionysus had travelled the length and breadth of the world, from Thrace to India, leaving his mark wherever he went.

Divine Dionysus — one of the oldest of gods: a horned god, whose head is wreathed in serpents, entwined with ivy, who transforms himself into Lion, Horse, Serpent and Bull. The storytellers sing of this most gentle and most terrible of gods. He was the god of ritual dance and sacred mysticism, of poetry, drama and wine. He was a god of bliss and ecstasy, but also of savagery; flesh-eating, demonic. He was a bull-horned god of fertility and male potency, yet slender as a woman. He was a god of the

mountains, wild and untamed, yet also generous and the bringer of gifts. It could be a description of Alexander. Almost.

Dionysus was a twice-born; first of an illicit union between Zeus and Semele, and then born again from the thigh of Zeus, who had hidden him there from the jealous eyes of his wife, the goddess Hera. Alexander would have called him brother, as he too believed he was born of Zeus.

Wine was Dionysus' gift to man. But wine was sometimes the enemy — as it was also for Alexander who, for all his genius of command and military strategy, was still a young man of only 25. Now he would collect a further scar on his reputation.

After a battle success in Sogdiana, at a celebration feast to Dionysus, there was a quarrel and another act committed — this time unforgivable, even to Alexander himself. Again, as at Persepolis, drink was the instigator; drink released the tongue and allowed home truths to be voiced; drink revealed all the suppressed anger against Alexander.

THE DEATH
OF CLEITUS

"Black" Cleitus, one of Alexander's oldest friends and foster brother, who had saved his life at Granicus, picked a drunken quarrel with Alexander. He began to sneer at Alexander's achievements; he suggested they were commonplace, and nothing compared to his father, Philip's.

While Cleitus continued to insult him, Alexander leaped to his feet and grabbed a spear. Others sprang to separate the two men. "What," taunted Cleitus, "am I a royal prince in name only? Am I to be like Darius, dragged around in chains by Bessus and his cronies?"

Cleitus was dragged from the hall before he could say anything worse,

but just when things were calming down, he reappeared, shouting and hurling insults. "Alexander! Is it thus that Greece repays her warriors? Shall one man claim the conquest won by thousands?" jeered Cleitus.

Provoked beyond endurance, his mind irrational with drink, Alexander hurled his spear deep into Cleitus' heart, and killed him on the spot.

The instant the deed was done, Alexander was struck with horror. He tried to kill himself by running onto his own sword, but was held back.

Howling and struggling, he was taken to his tent. There he lay for three days, refusing to see anyone, not eating or drinking, but weeping and blaming himself bitterly.

There had been nothing noble about the death of Cleitus. He had not been a traitor, he had not died on the field of battle or in equal combat. He had died because of a drunken quarrel; because drink had befuddled both of them, and distorted all judgement and principle. Cleitus had died shamefully in front of guests at a feast, by the hand of his own friend and brother, Alexander.

He was no god at this moment, but a man, who was too feeble to stand up to the effects of the wine of Dionysus.

Priests and seers looked for omens and evidence that the gods had forgiven Alexander, and only when they finally reassured him did he emerge to face the world.

PROSKYNESIS:
THE PERSIAN
KISS

Here among the dusty plains and brown mountains of Central Asia, so far from home, it seemed to many that Alexander was forgetting his own Greek culture. Murmurings of discontent rippled among his officers. Worst of all, Alexander insisted

on introducing yet another Persian custom — one which profoundly disgusted them. This was the custom of proskynesis: Persians who came before their king always prostrated themselves. The king then raised them to their feet with a kiss. Alexander liked this custom. But it was deeply offensive to the Greeks, going against their democratic principles.

Callisthenes, the historian and a nephew of Aristotle, spoke for them all, and made a speech denouncing Alexander for taking on foreign ways.

Alexander suggested a compromise. "Perhaps only Persians need prostrate themselves," he said.

But Callisthenes was scornful:

"Just because we are in a foreign land, are we therefore expected to think foreign thoughts? Alexander! I beseech you to remember Greece. Was it not for Greece that you undertook this campaign, to add Persia to her empire? And have you thought about what you will do when you go home? Will you really expect Greeks — who love freedom more than anything else in the world — to fall to the ground and prostrate themselves before you? Or will you perhaps exempt the Greeks and only insist on Macedonians performing this shameful act? Or you could let off the Greeks and the Macedonians, and make a broader distinction, and insist that only barbarians follow this barbarous custom, so that Greeks and Macedonians may be permitted to respect you honourably as a man!"

Alexander accepted the criticism, but only made small concessions. He kept the custom of proskynesis, though not enforcing it among his own officers. He continued involving the Persians in his administrations,

often giving them high positions which caused great jealousy, and unrest continued among the officers.

Soon after, there was another plot against Alexander's life, which almost succeeded. It involved the young sons of noblemen whose job was to protect Alexander. Instead, three or four of them plotted to kill him one night.

He had been drinking again and, on his way back to his tent, encountered a strange wild woman who told fortunes. "Don't sleep in your tent tonight, Alexander," she warned. Heeding her warning, he went back to the drinking party, and so the young men who had decided to kill him that night in his tent, waited in vain.

In the morning, one of the youths confessed and, under torture, another cited Callisthenes as the instigator.

Callisthenes had continued to criticize Alexander, but there was no proof he had plotted against him. Only the word of a terrified youth.

Perhaps Alexander was looking for an excuse to be rid of his critical historian. At any rate, Callisthenes was imprisoned and executed. It was an act which enraged Athens, who found Alexander's behaviour outrageous; Callisthenes was a respected historian, a nephew of Aristotle, and had been with Alexander from the beginning. His dispatches home had kept the Athenians in touch with the campaigns.

Even Alexander's admirers murmured, "Surely this act was ill-advised."

It was the winter of 328–327 BC when Alexander met Roxane.

ROXANE

There had been two years of bloody struggle for the outer

reaches of Iran. Two years, in which there had been wholesale massacres; ignoble acts combined with acts of mythic heroism. Alexander's character and charisma was such that he had the loyalty and devotion of his men – despite everything that had happened – for no matter what the criticisms whispered among the officers, his men still loved him and would do whatever he asked of them.

With him they had encountered princes and kings, made pacts, built cities and seen strange things too – like fire bursting out of the ground from wells which contained not water, but a substance unknown to them – oil. They had fought bloody and extraordinary fights; had campaigned through a winter of blizzards and thunderstorms, with hail and thunderbolts, when soldiers had frozen to death, their bodies welded into tree trunks against which they had leaned in exhaustion.

But there were still powerful kingdoms which did everything they could to repel Alexander's advance. Although most of Sogdiana was under his command, there was a last stronghold being defended by several hundred natives. It was on a huge rock plateau known as the Rock of Sogdiana, which everyone considered to be impregnable.

The snow was still thick on the ground. The pass they needed to go through was held by a powerful Sogdian baron called Oxyartes, whose warriors were encamped on the top the rock which was three miles high and fifteen miles round. Many nobles and their families had gone there for safety, including the wife and daughters of Oxyartes.

The whole rock was thickly guarded at the base and at the top, and it did indeed look impossible. Alexander tried to bargain with Oxyartes; a safe passage in exchange for accepting surrender. But Oxyartes just

laughed and mocked saying, "Go and find troops with wings!"

Never one to resist a challenge, Alexander said to his men, "We may not be able to fly, but we can climb." He offered any man who could reach the top twelve talents – a fabulous sum of money to a common soldier. Three hundred men stepped forward.

They then undertook an astonishing feat of mountaineering. Secretly, they found the sheerest part of the rock, which was unguarded and, with ropes and iron tent pegs, in the middle of a winter's night, they hauled themselves up the rock. 30 men perished, slipping to their deaths, but, as dawn was breaking, 270 men reached the top and stood on a pinnacle above the enemy camp. They fluttered linen flags to signal their success to Alexander.

Alexander yelled up to his enemy. "See! I found men who could fly!"

When the Sogdians looked up and saw the men, they thought that Alexander had miraculously flown his entire army to the top, so they fled or surrendered.

Oxyartes was captured, as were his daughters, including one called Roxane.

But it wasn't over yet. There was another rock to be taken. Alexander moved on and came to a deep ravine. Again he was taunted by the enemy. There was no way across. But his men felled trees day and night for his engineers to build a bridge – a sight these Sogdians had never seen before. Once again, Alexander defied the "barbarians" and nature, and marched relentlessly across to the other side.

The Sogdians fought bitterly; arrows and catapults soared over the ravine, but landed harmlessly on Greek and Macedonian shields. On

and on they battled, and would have fought to the death, but Oxyartes persuaded them to give up and enter into a pact with Alexander instead.

High up in the mountain fortress of Oxyartes, Alexander enjoyed a victor's feast. It must have been a wondrous affair, for Oxyartes had stored a vast amount of provisions in his stronghold, enough, he boasted, to feed Alexander and his men for two years.

At the feast, the Sogdian captives were paraded before him, among them, Roxane – "Little Star". Everyone who saw her declared her to be the most beautiful woman in Asia.

Although Alexander had the friendship and influence of many powerful women in his life from his own mother, Olympias, to Darius' mother, Sisygambis, and though he had met hundreds of beautiful and eligible women, none had ever fired his passion before. But at the banquet, when his eyes settled on Roxane, it was as if he had been struck by cupid's arrow. Overwhelmed with emotion, for the first time in his life, he fell in love with a woman. He ordered a marriage immediately.

The wedding feast was lavish in the Iranian style, but the marriage was Macedonian.

Alexander ordered bread to be brought in, according to Macedonian custom. The bread was cut with a sword, and each spouse ate off it, symbolizing not just the union of a man to a woman, or a king to a captive girl, but the union of Europe and Asia.

The music and dancing was wild and extraordinary; warriors leaped and stamped to an accompaniment of twirling women singing and clapping.

However, the Greeks and Macedonians would not have been pleased

at this union. They already hated Alexander's love of all things foreign. Now it seemed the heir to the Greek Empire, when he was born, would be half barbarian.

Much had changed since Alexander had left Macedonia full of ambition, with Achilles in his mind and Homer in his pocket. He had gloriously marched into the greatest civilizations in the known world, Ephesus, Babylon, Memphis, Persepolis, defeating the greatest empire in the world – the Persian. He had founded cities – at least seven of them – all called Alexandria. Greeks and Macedonians were brought in to live in them, bringing with them Greek culture and religion. He founded a new generation of soldiers, drawn from mixed marriages. He had moved far beyond Aristotle's belief that anyone who wasn't a Greek was a barbarian, to be regarded as merely a species of flora or fauna. He not only admired many other cultures and races, he knew that without the involvement of the people he had conquered, the empire could not be sustained.

Alexander thought deeply about his relationships with the gods, but his murder of Cleitus must have seemed proof enough that he was just a man after all. Was he still driven by his reputed ancestry with Zeus Ammon and Melkart *and* with Heracles who, it was said, had gone to India, as had Dionysus? Perhaps, to wipe out the stain of his human weakness for wine; perhaps to prove his lineage to the gods; or perhaps out of sheer curiosity, Alexander wanted to go on.

Alexander knew that in 516 BC Darius I had taken the Indian city, Gandara, and made it part of the Persian Empire, and that was enough for him. If India had been part of the Persian Empire, then it must be part of

his empire, even though Indian rulers had long since taken the area back and created kingdoms for themselves along the upper Indus River. He also remembered that Aristotle had told him the end of the world was somewhere beyond the river Indus in India. Perhaps, thought Alexander, he could reach the very ends of the earth.

THE CITIZENS
OF NYSA

Between the rivers of the Cophen and the Indus, inside the very edges of India, he came to the city of Nysa, and would have crushed it, but its leaders came out to meet him.

Alexander's reputation had gone before him; his deeds of destruction, terror and heroism put fear into the hearts of those who heard he was coming. They knew a fight with Alexander meant annihilation. So the citizens of Nysa sent a deputation of their leaders to request an audience.

The leaders arrived at Alexander's camp still amidst a melee of confusion following battles with local tribesmen. They were taken to Alexander's tent and ushered in.

Expecting to see him like some golden Persian king, seated in luxury, surrounded by slaves, they found him instead sitting in a modest tent alone, motionless, exhausted from battle. His limbs were unwashed and dust-stained, his helmet still on his head and his spear in hand. Speechless, they prostrated themselves before him. For a long time, no word was spoken.

The strange silence went on and on. Who could tell what Alexander was thinking? Had they come across him in a moment of indecision, weariness, homesickness, filled with horror at the enormity of his destruction even? Did he wonder what he was doing there? Why he was

fighting? Did he wish to turn back? But back to where? To his own small country of Macedonia? Back to Athens, where he knew he was as much despised as admired? Or was he such a wandering warrior, that his tent had become his home – wherever it was pitched?

Was he thinking of his new wife, Roxane, now pregnant with their child? Was he worrying about Hephaistion who, at that moment, had gone ahead and taken another route to India, to make contact with the Rajah of Taxila? In such terrain, surrounded by enemies, no one could guarantee a safe return.

Did the good citizens of Nysa strengthen his resolve to take on India? At any rate, they chose exactly the right argument to get Alexander on their side, for when at last he bade them rise to their feet, this is what they told him.

"The city of Nysa was founded by Dionysus after he had conquered India and was on his way home to Greece. He built it as a memorial to his long journey and his victories, and left there those men who were also his priests but who were no longer fit for service. He did what you too have done, sire. You founded Alexandria in the Caucasus and Alexandria in Egypt, and many others too, and you will surely found even more, thus exceeding the achievements of Dionysus himself. Sire, we request, that out of reverence for Dionysus, you leave us free and independent. Dionysus named this city Nysa, after his nurse, and the mountain nearby, Merus – meaning Thigh – as Dionysus was born from the thigh of Zeus. Ever since that time, Nysa has been free, and we have made our own laws and lived as good men. If you want proof that Dionysus was here and founded us, go forth and look about you. This is the only place in India where ivy

grows."

Alexander and his men did indeed find woods full of ivy — and animals too — and they went hunting, and held a feast at which they sang songs of Dionysus, and made sacrifices, and the Macedonian officers made themselves crowns of ivy and danced themselves into a frenzy. And so Alexander left the citizens of Nysa in peace.

Dionysus had gone to India and, the storytellers said, so had Heracles. Alexander could have had no doubt that he was destined to follow.

But though he must have remembered the adventures and feats of his fellow gods, his military mind — his enquiring mind — was still immensely practical, and he found out everything he could about the India he was about to enter, and what politics dominated the land before him.

He took his armies into the lower reaches of the Himalayas, concluding truces where he could, but subduing others who refused to co-operate.

Tales of his savagery and almost miraculous exploits spread. They told of how he built bridges, crossed canyons, gorges and rushing rivers; that he could even fly. He used incredible weapons like catapults and slings and siege techniques. His reputation was as fearsome as Rostam's.

India was next.

CHAPTER EIGHTEEN

INDIA

They stand on a peak of the Hindu Kush, the lower ranges of the Himalayas looking across to India, and are awestruck.

After the wide dusty plains of Central Asia, it seems they gaze upon the land of the gods – with snow-covered, forested mountains higher than Olympus. With breathtaking beauty, the sun rises and sets among the glistening peaks, and they wonder, entranced, about the magical kingdoms of the air; of the heavens of Vishnu and Shiva; of sky cities inhabited by sky demons, and of Surya, the sun god, who gallops across the sky each day in his golden chariot, pulled by five horses. And down below in the bowels of the earth, they hear of the dragons and serpents, and the red-eyed, flesh-eating demons. Alexander must have loved the stories of Krishna who, like Achilles, would die from an arrow piercing the only part of his body which could cause his death – the ankle.

Listen to the thunder. Remember the thunder gods Thor, Ra and Adad. In India it is Indra, Lord of Heaven, the mighty Bringer of Rain,

the Battler with Drought Demons, the Slaughterer of Enemies, the God of War. That mighty crash is his iron axe, smiting rocks, sending out brilliant flashes of light and sparks.

Indra had a son called Arjuna, a mighty hero who was one of the Pandava brothers fighting their cousins, the Kauravas. Krishna, a god on earth, tried to be an intermediary. With jangling bells and crashing cymbals, the dancers whirl out with faces painted black, red, green and white. Their wide embroidered skirts swirl as they stamp and dance, while the narrator calls out stories from the Mahabharata.

THE HATRED THAT LED TO WAR

Surya, the sun god, fell in love with the Princess Kunti. He covered her with his golden light and held her in his arms. In time, she bore his child. The shame was terrible. How could she say how it happened? So secretly, in the dead of night, Princess Kunti crept down to the riverbank carrying a cradle in which lay her newborn son – a son of Surya. Sorrowfully, she put the basket into the river and watched it float away. How fervently she prayed to the gods to protect him.

A charioteer, bathing in the river, saw the basket. He hooked it in, and finding a baby boy, was full of joy. He and his wife had prayed for children. They agreed this must be a gift from the gods, and named him Karna.

Later, Princess Kunti married the great King Pandu and was mother to his five sons. These sons became known as the Pandavas. King Pandu had only taken the throne because his elder brother, King Dhritarashtra, was blind. But there was bitterness in the kingdom, for King Dhritarashtra had 100 sons known as the Kauravas and, although the Pandavas and the Kauravas were brought up as brothers, being educated together and learning all the skills of princes, the rivalry between them was great. Whatever they learned, whether it was archery, sword fighting, horse riding or hunting, it was always the five Pandava brothers who outshone their cousins, and the Kauravas became very jealous.

One day, a magnificent tournament was held. Everyone in the land was invited, and the finest warriors came to take part. Once again, the Pandava brothers showed off their skill and bravery. It seemed no one could match them. Then a stranger appeared in golden armour. He marched up to Arjuna, the finest of the Pandava brothers and challenged him.

"Any skill you have, I have. I can do better. Look!"

The stranger took up his bow, aimed at an eagle in and let fly the arrow. The eagle plunged to earth. "See? And I aimed at his left eye!"

The Kauravas cheered. At last someone had come who could challenge the Pandavas.

"What is your name?" they asked.

"Karna," replied the stranger.

"What are you doing here?" asked the Pandava, Arjuna, suspiciously. "Who invited you?"

"Isn't this contest open to all?" retorted the stranger.

"What is your line of birth?" asked Arjuna? I fight no one who is below me in birth. Who is your father? Who is your mother?" Karna silently lowered his head. "What? You do not know your mother's name?" sneered Arjuna. "I won't fight you."

"Not so fast!" cried the eldest Kaurava brother, Duryodhana, who hated and feared Arjuna. "I hereby give Karna part of my kingdom; the land of Anga. I declare him King of Anga."

Karna was full of gratitude. "How can I repay you?"

"Always be on my side," replied Duryodhana. Then he called out triumphantly to Arjuna, "Karna is now a king! Come! Fight with your equal. Let the contest begin! A fight to the death!"

At this point, the queen, who had been watching, turned pale. She recognized the golden mien of this youth. He was her son, son of Surya, and here he was about to fight to the death with his own brother and there was nothing she could do.

Suddenly, a ragged old man appeared. He ran towards Karna. "O my son! I've been searching everywhere for you."

The old man was grasped by the guards, and a Kaurava brother demanded, "Who are you?"

"I am just a humble charioteer, and Karna is my son," said the old man.

"Karna is your son?" they exclaimed in amazement. "Is it true?"

How the Pandavas jeered with derision. "Why, cousins, you have made a low caste driver's son, King of Anga!" Then the Pandavas and Kauravas flew at each other, striking blows and hurling insults.

"Whatever his birth, he is noble. How many of us know our true origins?" cried Duryodhana. "Karna is our friend and ally." He embraced Karna, and called him brother. "Tell me what you desire and you shall have it."

"All I wish is to fight Arjuna in a fair and equal combat," answered Karna.

Suddenly the sky both darkened and brightened. Thunder clouds rolled. Shafts of light pierced through like golden arrows blinding those below. It was Indra the Lord of Heaven, siding with Arjuna, and Surya the Sun God defending Karna. But before they could fight, the sun galloped from the skies, and it became too dark to fight.

"Son of a charioteer! Go find a bullock cart to drive," jeered Arjuna.

Karna shouted back, furiously. "You may reject me now, Arjuna, but I promise you, we will meet again. We will fight, and I will kill you."

The day came, when Yudhishtritha, the eldest of the Pandava brothers, became King of Kings. He married the beautiful and noble princess, Draupadi. Because the five Pandava brothers were so united, Draupadi was a wife to them all. But the Kauravas were embittered. They were sure that one of them should have inherited the throne.

However, their uncle, Sakuni, a cunning gambler who was also known as a cheat, had a plan to get back the kingdom. "Yudhishtritha may be a wise man, but he has one weakness. He loves to gamble. I will challenge him to a game — but watch! No one has more skill with the dice than I. I'll make him play for the highest stakes."

The Pandavas and the Kauravas gathered for the game.

Yudhishtritha played for the Pandavas. First he staked all his jewels to

Sakuni, and lost them, followed by his treasures, slaves, horses and cows, and even his brothers — and lost them all. Finally, to cries of horror, he staked Draupadi, his wife, and lost her!

Draupadi was dragged before them trembling. She tried to escape, but a Kaurava grabbed her back by her hair. She was enraged.

"Don't touch me with your filthy hands. Do you not know that a woman's hair is sacred?"

But still they taunted.

"Accept your fate, Draupadi," jeered Karna. "You have no husband. You are a slave. You are nothing."

"We've won!" declared the Kauravas. "Let's strip them naked so that the world can see the Pandavas for what they really are,"

One by one, the Pandava brothers were stripped. Then they demanded that Draupadi too be stripped.

"Please no!" wept Draupadi. "Neither the wind nor sun has ever seen me naked."

But they took hold of the end of her sari and began to unwind it.

Draupadi called upon the decency of the Kauravas, but they laughed. She called upon the god, Krishna, to save her dignity. Miraculously, as they unwound the sari from her body — on and on — there was no end to it.

Ravens cawed, asses brayed and a jackal howled disturbing the white-clad Brahmin priests at prayer. At the sound of such terrible omens, they cried, sorrowfully, "Swashti, Swashti! So be it: it is their karma their fate. Amen!" The old blind king and father of the Kauravas also heard the howling, and asked what it meant. When he heard how his sons had

humiliated Draupadi he was overcome with the shame. He knelt before Draupadi and begged her forgiveness. "Ask me whatever you will, and I will grant it," he said.

"Free me from slavery. Free my husband, Yudhishtritha, and his brothers, so that we can go forth and regain our fortunes by our own mighty deeds."

This wish was granted. Draupadi followed the Pandava brothers into exile in the forest, unbinding her hair as she went, swearing that her hair would fall loose until the Kauravas were slain. Only when her hands were steeped in their blood, would she tie up her hair again.

Hatred burned on both sides; most of all the hatred between Karna and Arjuna. They swore blood and vengeance, no matter how long it took.

Desperate to bring an end to bloodshed, Krishna secretly revealed to Karna the truth of his birth. "Your father is the sun god, Surya, and your mother is Kunti, mother of the Pandavas. Karna, you fight your own brothers! Now will you stop this war?"

Karna reacted bitterly. "My mother, Kunti, abandoned me to the river. I was found by a chariot driver who I have always called father, and his wife, mother. They loved me and cared for me, and nothing can change that. I promised friendship and loyalty to the Kauravas, and I cannot break that promise."

"Alas," cried Krishna, "then the war goes on. It means ruin. The earth will be disfigured by corpses, and the animals will howl at the blood-red sky. You will fight your brothers. Understand this, Karna, I am on the side of the Pandavas. I will be Arjuna's charioteer."

"Then we will both make the sacrifice," replied Karna, "and I know we

will meet again at the end of our journey." So Krishna and Karna parted never to meet again on this earth.

So began the battle of eighteen days.

A plain fluttering with flags from end to end was the battleground. Karna, with the Kauravas faced his brother, Arjuna and the Pandavas.

Lord Krishna held the reins of Arjuna's chariot horses. They both gazed down upon the field.

"Drive me between the lines so that I may view my enemies," said Arjuna.

Krishna gathered up the reins of the five horses as if they were the five senses, and galloped along the line. Arjuna recognized his kinsmen, his own flesh and blood, fathers, grandfathers, uncles, nephews, sons and grandsons. With a terrible shudder, the warrior's bow fell from his hand. "I have no stomach for this war," he cried. "Ah, Krishna, what must I do? I seek no victory. What victory could this be against my own kinsmen? O day of darkness! How have we come to this?"

Krishna answered, "What you see is not the truth. You are not fighting mortals, you are fighting evil, and you must win. Death is just throwing off an old garment to put on a new one. Trust me, Arjuna, for I, Krishna, am the Light!"

At each pale dawn, the warriors faced each other. At each red sunset, the battlefield was running with blood. Funeral pyres burned as bright as day. On the seventeenth day of the war, so many fathers and sons had died, including the young son of Arjuna. Heart-broken, Arjuna took on Karna in mortal combat.

Arjuna's arrows fell upon Karna like summer rain, but the arrows of Karna fell upon Arjuna like stinging snakes. Suddenly Arjuna's bow string was severed. He was unarmed and helpless. "Karna!" he called. "Remember the laws of combat. It is forbidden to strike a man without his weapon."

But Karna continued to fire arrows ruthlessly till Arjuna fell.

"Finish him off!" cried Karna. His charioteer tried to drive the chariot round, but a wheel got stuck in a rut. Arjuna hauled a crescent-bladed arrow from his sheath and flung it, striking off Karna's head.

With the Kauravas in disarray, the Pandavas thundered on, sweeping all before them. They took their revenge; drank the blood of their enemies, and danced on their entrails.

All 100 Kaurava brothers were dead. Draupadi, her hands dripping with the blood of those who had humiliated her, tied up her hair.

The war was over. Now, the Pandavas looked for purification. They made sacrifices and bathed in the sacred waters, they brought back peace and prosperity and waited for the day when, one by one, they would make their different ways to Heaven to be welcomed by Lord Krishna and Lord Indra.

Also waiting was Karna and the Kauravas. They embraced and wept for joy.

Here in the celestial city, finally purified they could at last forget their quarrel.

CHAPTER NINETEEN

TO THE ENDS OF THE EARTH

Hephaistion had already reached the River Indus and bridged it with a pontoon constructed by dozens of boats. It was sturdy enough to carry an army. He had successfully made a treaty with the Rajah of Taxila, who had given him many gifts of silver, sheep, oxen and elephants, including a contingent of men to join Alexander's forces. This was not just friendship, it was to have Alexander on his side against a rival rajah called Porus.

Leaving Roxane in Balkh to join him later in India, Alexander descended to the banks of the Indus. He was welcomed as conqueror and entered the capital of Taxila to be greeted by its rajah, Ambhi, and given a vast supporting army in return for retaining his kingdom.

Travelling round, exploring and familiarizing himself with the area, Alexander began to hear of new philosophies. He was fascinated by naked men with shaved heads, who the Greeks called "gymnosophistai," or naked philosophers, but who were priestly Brahmins. Painfully, through various translators, he tried to learn and understand. He had always loved

philosophy, and was constantly seeking out people with whom he could discuss ideas. So when he was introduced to a Hindu philosopher called Calanus, he was pleased to meet a man who he could talk to, listen to, and respect. Calanus in turn was fascinated by Alexander, who told him all about Greek ideas, systems and philosophies, and was persuaded to join Alexander's entourage. Their friendship was so great that Calanus stayed with Alexander throughout the rest of his campaigns.

Alexander's force was now enlarged by 6,000 infantry and 5,000 horsemen. With these troops, he marched towards the banks of the River Hydaspes which flowed between Taxila and the kingdom of the Rajah, Porus.

MONSOON

He lined them up on the banks of another big river, to fight another large scale classical battle.

But this was India. The monsoon had started.

Alexander didn't know about the monsoon. He had never been stopped by weather conditions before. His men had endured terrible heat, the extreme cold of mountains and desert – and plenty of rain – so warnings about Indian rain seemed unimportant.

He didn't know that the rainy season in India meant heavy lashing rain, without stopping, for three whole months. His armies became convinced that it would never cease. And then there were the snakes: huge poisonous snakes which the rains brought out from their crannies and hollows; snakes in the river, snakes hanging from the branches of trees, snakes in the undergrowth, little snakes who could hide in a slipper, and whose bite could kill within hours. So many of his soldiers would die from snake

bites. The land they had heard of in legend was full of wondrous jewels and fantastic customs; of naked holy men, and funeral pyres on which women willingly threw themselves. But the heat, the incessant rain, the discomfort, the insects and disease — and the snakes — they didn't expect these and were appalled.

However, there was a battle to be fought and, once again, Alexander rallied his men for Jehlum on the Hydaspes river.

The swollen river flows fast.

THE BATTLE
OF HYDASPES

The rain falls incessantly.

A wall of war elephants lines the riverbank, their unnerving trumpeting defying Alexander and his horses to cross. Behind the elephants, the Rajah Porus has lined his vast army of some 300 war chariots, 3,000 cavalry and as many as 50,000 infantry. They watch as Alexander roams up and down the riverbanks looking for a suitable crossing. Sometimes contingents of soldiers punt out on rafts, looking as if they might attack, but always out of bow-shot of the Indian archers.

Alexander was up to his old tricks again, taking his time, looking intermittently as if he was ready to attack, then looking indecisive, wearing down the enemy with puzzlement, boredom and complacency. Wagon-loads of food came to and fro into his camp, giving the impression that he was bedding down to wait for the end of the rainy season when it would be easier to cross the surging river.

But while Alexander distracted his enemy with all this activity, he himself was exploring up-river, looking for a suitable crossing place.

He reached a city called Jalalpur on the banks of the river, and there he saw an island in the middle, creating a narrow channel between it and the banks on either side. The island was heavily wooded with deep gullies — perfect for hiding an army.

Alexander set about further confusing his enemy. By day he created a sense of bustle and preparation as if his troops were preparing to attack. By night, he lit fires as though they were encamping till the rains had stopped. This went on day after day and night after night, so that one minute, Porus was braced for attack, and the next, relaxed, as he became convinced that Alexander couldn't get his army across the river during monsoon.

However, Alexander heard that Porus had sent for re-enforcements from another rajah, Abisares, and he knew he mustn't allow the two armies to join up against him. So at last he put his plan into action.

Under the command of one of his generals, Craterus, he left the bulk of his army openly in view of the enemy, even having a man dressed like himself to appear from time to time in the King's pavilion.

Meanwhile, secretly, and piecemeal, Alexander had his flotilla of boats carried up river to Jalalpur. With a force of 5,000 horses and 10,000 infantry, he took up position opposite the island, leaving Craterus with a second contingent to join him later, once Porus had been engaged in battle.

Alexander intended to attack from behind. When Porus turned in response, Craterus would, as instructed, cross the river and attack him from the front and break up his mighty war elephants. Porus would be caught in a deadly pincer, turning one way into Craterus, the other into Alexander.

Of course, it was impossible to keep such large troop movements secret for long. Indian scouts went galloping back to Porus to tell him that Alexander was crossing higher up river. Porus immediately dispatched a force of 2,000 horsemen and 120 chariots with archers, hoping to attack Alexander while he was crossing the river.

Headed by Porus' son, they rode as fast as they could, but arrived too late. The main body of Alexander's men had already crossed the river, and the Indians were no match for the Macedonian army. They were soon in disarray, heavily out-numbered, and out-fought. With their chariots bogged down in the monsoon mud, they fled, leaving 400 dead, including Porus' son.

Now Craterus was on the move and beginning to cross the river. Porus had to decide whom he should fight: Craterus or Alexander? Fatally, he chose to turn towards Alexander's contingent. He marched upstream with an army of about 20,000 infantry, 2,000 horses, 180 chariots and 130 elephants. They found a sandy plain where the earth was firmer and the chariots wouldn't flounder. His battle line stretched for four miles, divided into battalions of infantry each guarded by a war elephant in front. On each wing he stationed his cavalry masked by his war chariots.

As usual, Alexander had a plan: he would send a division led by one of his generals, Coenus to steal round the back of Porus' right wing where, out of sight, they would be ready to encircle him. Alexander would then attack the left wing. When Porus turned to meet this attack, Coenus would charge in across the enemy lines and attack them from behind. The other battalions – the phalanx and Guard Brigades – were instructed not

to attack until the Indian horse and foot soldiers had been thrown into confusion.

Now Alexander was ready. A thousand mounted archers launched themselves against the Indian left wing, overcoming most of Porus' chariots.

Alexander himself then charged into the centre, forcing Porus to do exactly what he wanted him to do. Sitting on the top of his royal elephant, Porus ordered his right wing division to come in.

With his fresh troops, Coenus broke cover and galloped in from the rear, trapping the Indians. The plan looked so clean and easy when drawn on paper or marked in the sand – but it was dreadful in reality. Wounded and maddened elephants crashed about as Alexander surrounded them, attacking them with spears and arrows, javelins and scimitars. The wounded elephants retaliated by stamping soldiers under foot, impaling them on their tusks, and hurling them to the ground with their trunks. In the confusion, Indian and Macedonian alike were trampled.

But unlike Darius, Porus didn't flee the field. He charged in on his elephant, even though it was futile. The Macedonians locked shields and closed in.

Then began the most fearful butchery. Crazed by the conditions; the blood, rain, mud and corpses, fleeing horses and maddened, trampling elephants, Alexander's men slaughtered thousands of Indians.

Rajah Porus fought to the bitter end, but at last, wounded and losing blood, he rode slowly away. Alexander chased after him on his horse and caught the Indian king, a man of heroic looks, seven feet tall, sitting on a giant elephant.

"How do you wish to be treated?" demanded Alexander.

"Like a king," replied Porus.

Alexander respected the valiant way Porus had fought and led his army. He left him in charge of his kingdom in return for an alliance with him.

So Jehlum was won.

DEATH OF
BUCEPHALUS

Roxane came to join Alexander, pregnant with their child. But there was sorrow, too. Alexander's wonderful, black horse that he had had since childhood, Bucephalus, his steed of the past thirteen years, his devoted companion who would let no one else ride him, was dead. Not because of wounds in battle – Alexander had always cared for him, and loved him as much as any living creature – but from exhaustion and age. He was 30 years old.

Once again, Alexander founded a city. This time, he called it Bucephala.

India was full of curiosities. Alexander was fascinated by its people, their forms of religion, their strange practices and extraordinary gods. There was so much to intrigue, mystify and disturb; so many mysteries and tales of magic, astrology and fortune-telling, interpreting every detail of life.

Alexander's teacher, Aristotle, had told him that somewhere beyond the Indus, he would come to the end of the world. He believed that the Indus joined up with the Nile, and that there was an ocean to the east – part of the great Stream of Ocean which he believed encircled the world. Alexander thought that if he could reach this ocean, he would be able to sail all the way back to Alexandria in Egypt, and then home.

But he still only had the vaguest idea of the size of India. If Aristotle

was right, the end of the world was just over the river. There, he had heard, was a vast expanse of water, which was the eastern ocean on which they could sail back to Egypt.

Fired with enthusiasm, his army now reinforced with 5,000 Indians and dozens of elephants, Alexander continued pushing further east, crossing rivers, and subduing cities. It was only when they arrived at the Hyphasis River that the truth became clear. To reach the ocean they must cross the river and endure a twelve-day trek across the Thar Desert.

But then Alexander learnt that the great expanse of water beyond the desert which he thought was the eastern ocean, was not the sea, but another river, the River Ganga, whose breadth at that point was three to four miles wide. Furthermore, on the other side of the Ganga was another hostile rajah to be fought. This was Rajah of Maghdah, head of the powerful Nanda dynasty, whose huge army included 2,000 chariots and 4,000 elephants. Alexander was beginning to realize that India stretched on and on. Porus had told him about other fabulous empires to be conquered. More explorer now than military leader, Alexander was curious. He wanted to go on.

Alexander's men were aghast. For the first time since they had left home, there were serious murmurings of discontent.   DISCONTENT
Sullenly, they made it clear they did not want to go any further.

Alexander tried to encourage and inspire them. "Are we to go home just to sit in comfort, guarding our houses, and doing nothing more than repelling a few tribes on our borders? We have come further than Heracles. Look how much we have conquered. Come now, and add the rest of Asia to what you already possess. Those of you who want to go

home, go, but those of you who stay with me will have riches beyond any ambition and will be the envy of those who return."

His men were unimpressed. They were utterly weary after eight years of continuous warfare and the endless slog across miles and miles of flat Indian plain. Their horses were footsore, the proud uniforms in which they had started out, had long ago fallen into tatters, and they were forced to wear thin Indian garments. They felt like ragamuffins. Worst of all, they had endured rain, rain, rain. The monsoon had washed away all their vitality, and snakes and disease had tested their loyalty to the utmost. Stubbornly, they refused to go on.

When Alexander heard their grumbling, he lost his temper. "All right, go home!" he shouted at them. "Go home and tell everyone how you abandoned Alexander in the midst of his enemies," and he stomped away to sulk in his tent, as Achilles had once done.

It wasn't a mutiny. No one wanted to overthrow him. They just didn't want to go on, and Coenus bravely put the men's point of view to Alexander.

He reminded him of what the men had endured; death in battles, wounds, disease; of how many had been abandoned on the trail, and of those left unwillingly in the new colonies. They had been away for eight years, far away from their families, Coenus told him, and they all longed for home.

The next morning, Alexander relented. He knew the men would go no further, and that he had used up their loyalty. He agreed to turn back.

The men wept and cheered.

The moment Alexander made the decision to turn back, was also the

moment when he realized that he would never reach the ends of the earth, or know everything there was to know. For Alexander, the explorer, his curiosity unquenched. It was a bitter decision.

When Alexander returned to Jehlum, there was more to dispirit him and make him wonder if the gods had abandoned him. Roxane had lost her baby, and now he began to hear of other omens: omens of death.

One day, he came across some holy wise men, naked and covered in ash, stamping their bare feet on the ground. When he asked what was the meaning of this strange behaviour, they replied: "King Alexander, a man can only own as much of the earth's surface as the piece beneath his feet. You are human, like the rest of us, but always busy and up to no good, travelling so many miles from your home, being a nuisance to yourself and others. Ah well! You will soon be dead, and will only need as much ground as it takes to bury you."

He was told of a garden with talking trees; trees that were like oracles and foretold the future. Alexander wanted to know more, and was taken to a sanctuary garden, where they told him that in the middle of the garden, dedicated to the Moon and the Sun, stood two trees — rather like cypresses, but with strange nuts and fruit. One tree was the Sun and spoke with a man's voice, the other spoke with a woman's voice, and was the Moon. They said that the tree of the Sun spoke prophecies three times a day, at dawn, at noon and at sunset, and that the Moon tree spoke at night, on rising, at its zenith and on setting. Alexander was curious to hear these voices. Perhaps they would tell him something important.

He could enter the sanctuary garden, they said, if he removed all metal

from his person.

Alexander took off his sword, breastplate and all other metal, and went into the sanctuary with Indian interpreters, warning them that if the trees didn't speak, he would have them burned alive.

From sunrise to sunset, he stood near the Sun tree and heard nothing. But just as the last rays of the sun was sinking below the horizon, a man's voice spoke from within the tree.

The Indian interpreters looked flustered and afraid, and didn't want to translate the words.

"What did he say?" demanded Alexander anxiously.

At last one Indian whispered in his ear. "Alexander, you will soon die by the hand of one of your own companions."

At this disturbing news, Alexander wanted to hear the second tree speak, and to ask whether he would ever see his mother again. So he waited for the moon to rise.

The Moon tree spoke to him in Greek. "King Alexander! You will die in Babylon, by the hand of one of your own companions, and you will never see your mother again, and when you die, she, Roxane and your heir will be murdered."

When Alexander heard this, he was filled with deep melancholy and made plans to leave India at once.

CHAPTER TWENTY

THE JOURNEY BACK

But one thing was certain; Alexander's retreat would not be ignominious. If he couldn't continue further into India, then he would take a different route back, exploring the Hydaspes river instead till it met the Indus, from where he would follow it to the ocean. How wonderful, if he could establish a sea route from India to Persia.

He set his men to work felling trees. Within two months, they had built a whole fleet of boats: triremes for the men, 30-oared boats for the officers, flat-bottomed boats for the horses, and others for grain and supplies as well as a variety of craft required to take the women, children and all the other camp followers.

The boats were lavishly decorated and their sails were purple. So extraordinary a sight was it, that the local people ran alongside them for miles, while the rhythmic chants of the rowers echoed among the rocks and gorges. Alexander's men sang joyfully. At last, they were on a homeward journey.

But for Alexander, who would be lucky to leave India alive, there was still time for more myth-making. They were constantly fighting skirmishes with tribal groups, and by this time, the monsoon was over, and the exhausting heat was back with a vengeance.

As they negotiated the different twists and turns of the river, they came near the territory of the Malloi, a fearsome tribe.

The Malloi had a fortress dominating the River Ravi, along which Alexander must pass. He insisted it must be captured. Even though it didn't seem altogether necessary, the troops responded to Alexander's call to arms. He praised their courage, invoked his heroic image as son of Zeus, the invincible, and downplayed the numerous defeats and setbacks they had suffered in India. Before, after many previous low points, the troops had always rallied to his call. They did so again, with eagerness, begging him to lead them on with the help of heaven.

THE MASSACRE
AT MULTAN

He led them on a detour across a muddy desert, they stormed a fortress and a town on the way, until at last they reached Multan, the stronghold of the Malloi. Alexander's soldiers were outnumbered by more than ten to one.

Many of them had joined the army under his father, Philip, over twenty years before. They had known no other life, and now, under Alexander, had grown old; many were in their sixties. Yet, though exhausted from their campaigns, and suffering from the appalling conditions of India, they breached the outer walls, and headed for the inner citadel, inspired by Alexander's youth and energy.

Speed was of the essence. Where were the ladders? Always first into the fray, Alexander seized the nearest ladder, and climbed to the top.

He was an extraordinary sight; this handsome, fair, godlike man, with flowing locks, with his shining breastplate and sword in hand. Behind him came his shield-bearer, carrying the shield of Achilles, with which he had travelled all the way from Troy.

His soldiers surged forward and tried to follow him up the ladder, causing it to collapse under the weight of their numbers. Alexander and his three attendants were stranded. Taken by surprise, the Malloi poured out. What should Alexander do? Should he jump backwards to be saved by his friends, or forwards into the arms of his enemies?

We speak of Alexander! Believing in his own myth as son of Zeus — a god-king, he hurled himself forwards among his enemies, who instantly fell upon him. The arrows flew; his attendants were wounded. Alexander lunged and thrust with his sword, keeping them at bay, while missiles thudded all around. He was encircled. An enemy arrow pierced his corselet and penetrated his chest. Surely this was the end for him! An Indian leaped forward to finish him off. With one last desperate lunge, Alexander stabbed him with his sword, then fell back with blood spurting from his wound, while his desperate attendant held the shield of Achilles over him as protection.

By this time, the Macedonians had smashed through the gates and walls, and were pouring in, bellowing war cries. Seeing their stricken Alexander, they were enraged, and fought with passion, hatred and vengeance. Alexander too struggled on, till, fainting with the loss of blood, he finally collapsed over his shield.

Believing that their king had been mortally wounded, his men massacred every single man, woman and child. The price for killing a king.

They carried Alexander back to camp. Messages flew. Hephaistion, leading the advance party, was told Alexander was dead. The arrow had pierced his lung.

But Alexander did not die. His skillful Greek physician removed the arrow and staunched the blood. Hurriedly, he was carried to the boat and taken downstream to where a grief-stricken Hephaistion was waiting.

He expected a corpse, but as the boat neared the river bank, Alexander raised an arm to wave, and the army cheered with relief. They wanted to take him from the boat to a bed, but Alexander said it must be to his horse. When his men saw him mounted, again they cheered and wept. To show he was very much alive, Alexander dismounted from the horse and walked unaided to his tent. His men, who had been terrified that they were leaderless among hostile tribes, reached out to touch him and shower him with flowers, reassured and grateful that Alexander would live.

Tales of the massacre at Multan spread, but to Alexander's advantage. This was the land of the Mahabharata; of the Pandavas and Kauravas, with tales of the bloodiest of battles, revenge and heroism. Either from fear or admiration – or both – the locals came pouring in with lavish and wonderful gifts of jewels and elephants. Banquets were held, and the hospitality was royal.

For two weeks Alexander recuperated. At last, though suffering immense pain, he continued by boat, still organizing, ruling, handing out territories, building dockyards, and even founding another Alexandria.

It was in mid-July 325 BC that Alexander reached the city of Pattala at the mouth of the Indus. As usual, he was full of activity and plans. While

Hephaistion and his men built a fort, a shipyard and more ships, Alexander explored the upper reaches of the tributaries which poured into the Indus, and then followed the Indus river down to the Indian Ocean, making constant sacrifices and libations to the gods. He was sure that he was about to discover a new sea route which would link India with the rest of the world.

At last he was ready for the next leg of the journey home. He split up his army into three sections. The first group led by his general, Craterus, was instructed to take his men and elephants overland to the Persian Gulf, via Arachosia and Drangiana and through the Bolan Pass to Carmania, near the Straits of Hormuz, where they would wait for Alexander.

INTO THE
MAKRAN DESERT

The second group would go by boat, following the Indus down to the sea, and sailing on to the Persian Gulf.

Alexander would go with the third group, a contingent of soldiers and hundreds of camp followers, who would follow the fleet along the shore. They would keep the ships supplied with food and water until they reached the Persian Gulf. This could be the start of a major trade route, opening up the wealth and riches of India to the rest of the world.

But Alexander's decision to take the shore route meant that it would be one of the most unpleasant and near fateful journeys of his entire life, for it would take him into the Makran Desert. No army had ever come through this desert successfully, neither the legendary Queen of Babylon, Semiramis who, came back from India with only twenty survivors, nor even King Cyrus who came back with only three.

"Don't go," he was urged by his advisers. "It is absolute folly."

But the more they told him how dangerous it was, the more Alexander

was deaf to their advice. After all, he was Alexander, the explorer, a descendant of Heracles, obsessed with the challenge of finding the new; unwilling to listen to any talk of obstacles.

It is October 325 BC.

Craterus begins his long journey overland, the fleet sets sail down the coast under the command of Nearchus, one of Alexander's most trusted generals, and Alexander himself, with some thousands of men, women and children, keeps pace with the ships along the shore, never straying more than twenty miles from the sea.

They enter the Makran Desert.

It is impossible to describe the ordeal and the appalling hardship they began to endure. It was so hot they could only move at night – but then they endured freezing temperatures which dropped to below 35 degrees. The ground was not firm beneath their feet, but deep, soft, sifting sand which sucked the energy out of their every step. If they reached a watering place, the men were so desperate they often gulped the water till they bloated up and were then sick, and many died. As their food ran out, those who had been ordered to get supplies to the fleet often just tore into them for themselves once they were out of sight.

Ridge after ridge of sand dunes rose and fell like waves on a never-ending ocean, without any landmarks or characteristic features. Even the native guides got lost, and they wandered deeper inland. It was left to Alexander to set off with some men and regain the coast.

The route was utterly arid and there was no food or water for them, let alone to supply the ships at sea. Soon, hundreds were dying from

exhaustion, heat, thirst and starvation, and hundreds more were lost, or perished among the drifting sand dunes. Flash floods washed away one camp, while poisonous plants killed their animals. They encountered strange fish-eating tribes who seemed barely human who scavenged along the coast, and stank from eating raw fish; who used their long curling fingernails, which they never cut, to poke out the goodness from molluscs and oysters. Alexander and his men tried to do the same, but were nauseated. And even here, there were snakes.

But there are stories of heroism; once when a small amount of water was found, it was given first to Alexander. Like the rest of them, he was tormented by thirst, but he poured it away into the sand saying, "Either we all drink, or none of us does." And though his wound must have troubled him every inch of the way, he refused any special privileges.

Finally they found a route which took them inland to kinder pastures, and, at last, to their rendezvous in Hormuz, where Craterus was waiting for them. Alexander had entered the desert with 12,000 people, it took them 60 days to reach their destination, and more than a third did not come out alive. It was a disaster, but somehow Alexander survived with his reputation intact.

When the news spread that he had come through alive, people were amazed. Once more, he had lived up to his legend, and re-enforced the belief that he was godlike.

Meanwhile Nearchus and his men had also had their problems; the fleet ran into storms; there were tales of strange spouting sea creatures, which they saw on their voyage, not realizing they were whales. Without the food and water Alexander was supposed to supply them with, they

had had to go foraging for food along the coast. They had skirmished with hostile tribes, met the fish-eaters along the coast, and were reduced to looking like a starved rabble.

Nearchus and a group of men finally left the ships and set off across land to try and rendezvous with Alexander. So bedraggled and wild did they look that they were unrecognized by a group of scouts Alexander had desperately sent out looking for them. They had already passed each other on the road, when a scout overheard one of them speak in Greek. Only then did they realize who they were, and embraced each other with tears of joy and relief.

At last, after ten weeks at sea, the fleet entered the Straits of Hormuz. A relieved Alexander welcomed them with games, music and feasting.

CHAPTER TWENTY-ONE

THE RETURN TO PERSIA

In January 324 BC with his army united again, Alexander marches back into Persia. It is like returning to paradise.

He retraced his steps back to Persia's softer landscapes. He went back to Persepolis and, standing among the bleak ruins, soberly contemplated the terrible destruction. Realizing that he had destroyed something without parallel, he expressed remorse. Moving on to Pasagarde, he paused and took the time to restore the tomb of Cyrus, almost as act of repentance.

Then it was onwards – to Susa.

As they approached Susa, Calanus, the Hindu philosopher, fell ill. Calanus, who had joined Alexander in Taxila, and stayed with him all the way through his battles in India and the trek back to Persia, was an old man – 73 years old and, though he had never been ill before, the chill of a Persian winter brought on sickness. He told Alexander

THE DEATH OF
CALANUS

he had no wish to be an invalid and that the time had come for him to die. He asked that his funeral pyre be constructed.

Alexander was aghast and did all he could to persuade his friend not to think this way. But Calanus was adamant. "You may be able to compel a body to do your will, but a soul you cannot compel, any more than you can make bricks and stones talk."

Everyone turned out to see this extraordinary funeral procession. His way strewn with flowers, Calanus was carried on a garlanded litter, singing Hindu hymns. He was taken to the funeral pyre, where, unaided, he climbed up and settled himself on his death bed signalling for the fire to be lit. His last mysterious words to Alexander were, "I'll see you in Babylon."

The flames flared up, the bugles sounded, elephants trumpeted and the whole army roared war cries as Calanus was engulfed without emitting a single sound.

All around him, the empire Alexander had conquered was teetering.

In his absence, there had been insurrection, corruption and many of the men he had left in charge had been murdered. Alexander knew only too well that an empire couldn't be held together without the involvement and co-operation of its citizens. So it was at Susa that he not only took two more wives — one, Stateira, the daughter of Darius, and the other a daughter of the previous king, Artaxerxes — but he held a fabulous mass wedding at which 2,000 of his officers were ordered to marry Persian girls.

Hephaistion married another of Darius' daughters, so that his children and Alexander's would be linked by blood.

Never had there been such lavish celebrations. No expense was spared; there were sumptuous bridal suites, banquets, entertainments, music and drama. The weddings were conducted with full solemnity of Persian tradition. All the wives were given dowries and full Greek status and their children were to be given a Greek-style education – the boys to be trained into Alexander's future army.

Alexander's aim was to unite Persians, Macedonians and Greeks within his empire; but despite all his efforts, the Greeks and Macedonians still loathed the Persian way of life and deeply resented the customs which had been forced on them. Roxane's brothers had been elevated to high positions and it seemed that Alexander was discriminating against his own kind.

It was the autumn of 324 BC. Alexander had moved to the city of Opis, trying to consolidate his kingdom. The seething discontent culminated when a large contingent of young Persian men arrived to take part in army drill in full Macedonian military dress. Their presence unsettled the Greeks and Macedonians. They wondered jealously if they were about to be sidelined.

Alexander was heavily criticized by his hardcore of ageing veterans in particular, so he decided to retire them and send REBELLION them home. Insulted and humiliated the grumblings surged into open protest, even though Alexander told them what generous pensions they would receive. The old officers rebelled, and the rest of the army supported them.

It was the closest Alexander ever came to facing an all-out mutiny from the rank and file.

[215]

He stood on a platform trying to exert his authority and explain his policies, but his men surged forward angrily.

"If you send the veterans home, then we'll all go."

The crowd was large now and in an ugly mood, taunting and booing. "Go on campaigning then with your father," they jeered.

"Father?" Did they mean Zeus? Who knows which taunt hit home, but as with the Malloi, Alexander, in a rage, leaped down among them — surely another act of pure folly. Any one of his men in that moment could have put the knife into him. But he strode among them, pointing out the main ringleaders and ordering them away to be executed as traitors. He then jumped back onto his podium and gave another of his pieces of oratory. Alexander could harangue, could rage, could sulk, but when he used his powers of persuasion, few could resist. If anything saved him on that day, it was the sheer force of his presence.

With their ringleaders dead, and faced with the prospect of going home without wages and pensions, his men were finally pacified and begged to be forgiven. Alexander kept them waiting. For several days they came to his door by night and day, swearing loyalty, until at last he came out to be reconciled with them. They wept and sang victory songs, many falling to their knees to kiss him in the Persian way.

The rebellion was over. With his usual sense of style and generosity, Alexander held a lavish banquet and forgave everyone.

The departure of his elderly generals was dignified and emotional. With honour satisfied on both sides, Alexander continued his journey on to the beautiful city of Hamadan, where he hoped to spend a leisurely autumn being entertained with music and theatre and games.

It was at one of these festivities that Hephaistion felt ill. He had a temperature and took himself off to bed. It didn't seem too serious and the games and festivites continued. Although his doctor put him on a strict diet, Hephaistion ignored him and ate a full meal washed down with a flagon of wine. His condition deteriorated dramatically. For the next seven days, he struggled with a high temperature, and Alexander stayed constantly in touch. On the eighth day, while Alexander was watching the boys racing at the games, word came that Hephaistion had suffered a dramatic relapse. Alexander hurried from the games, but arrived at his friend's bedside too late. Hephaistion was dead.

THE DEATH OF
HEPHAISTION

Appalled that he had not been with him, Alexander flung himself, sobbing, over his body. Not since the death of Cleitus had any of them seen such uncontrollable grief. For three days, he shut himself away, weeping and lamenting, unable to eat or sleep. No one on this earth had he loved more than Hephaistion, and it seemed that nothing – neither Roxane nor anyone else – had ever dented the strength of their love for each other. Only the stories he had heard of Achilles and Patroclus, Gilgamesh and Enkidu, or the father and son, Sohrab and Rostam, could have prepared him for the sorrow he would feel.

A period of mourning was ordered throughout the East, but Alexander was too upset to organize the funeral arrangements himself. Even so, it was a momentous, lavish occasion with no expense spared. The building of a fabulous chariot and monument was planned, to honour Hephaistion who, on consultation with the priests, was declared a god.

What real happiness was left to Alexander after the death of Hephaistion? If he had lost the will to live, it wasn't obvious.

By 323 BC he was at the peak of his fame, wealth and splendour; feared and admired as a conqueror and worshipped as a god. Roxane was pregnant again. He could look forward to the future, and for him the future seemed full of possibilities. He hadn't lost his passion for exploring and conquering the world, he was trying to consolidate trade and even making plans to go to those yet unvisited lands of the north – including Britain.

Yet there was something reckless in the way he was living; something ostentatious and excessive. He indulged in sumptuous banquets and long drinking bouts; he held constant games, with theatricals, music, poetry and dance. He loved being lavish and extravagant, often appearing dressed as a god, sometimes as Zeus Ammon, with horns on his head, and sometimes even dressed as Artemis, in female clothes.

Autumn ended. In the tradition of Persian kings, Alexander left Hamadan and rodes towards Babylon. He planned to spend the winter there. He was stopped on the way. Omens had predicted his death. His priests begged him not to enter the city. But Alexander took no notice. He intended that Babylon should be the capital of his empire.

PORTENTS OF DEATH

Still full of enthusiasm and energy, he pursued a huge programme of opening up trade, rebuilding the fleet and constructing new harbours. People might think of him only as a despot and a tyrant, but most tyrants simply destroy and move on. Alexander was different. His desire for power embraced a passion for building, establishing trade and exploring the world. He often took the helm of his boat, and sailed out across the lake and into the many rivulets among the marshes and reed beds around Babylon, planning ways of draining them and developing the city further. Among the many islands was one near which Icarus was reputed to have fallen, so Alexander named it "Icarus".

"Pay heed, Alexander," the soothsayers begged him. "Those who compete with the gods are doomed to lose! Think of Daedalus! In creating, he also killed! That is the lesson to be learned."

THE STORY OF DAEDALUS AND ICARUS

Daedalus was an amazing genius, a descendant of Hephaestus, a craftsman, a sculptor and an inventor. As a carpenter, Daedalus invented the lathe, the saw, the carpenter's compass; as an architect, he invented the plumb line, the gimlet and glue; as a sculptor he made statues that seemed alive. He constructed the maze for King Minos, and gave Ariadne a ball of thread which would lead her through the Minotaur's palace to rescue Prince Theseus.

Icarus was his beloved son. When King Minos discovered Daedalus had given away the secret of the maze, he ordered him and his son to be incarcerated in the labyrinth. But birds loved flying in and out of the labyrinth and Daedalus thought, "If only I too could fly and escape from here." An idea grew in his mind. Painstakingly, he gathered all the feathers he could find and glued them together with wax to make two pairs of wings for himself and his son. Then they prepared to fly to freedom.

"Be guided by the stars! Remember the reference points of sailors," he told his son. "Follow the constellations of Bootes, the Ox-herder, Ursa Major, the Great Bear, and Orion's Sword. Follow the straight route; the halfway point between high and low, as a carpenter guides his plane straight."

And so, one night, they leaped from the walls into space and flew. At first they followed the stars, but when dawn broke and the sun's chariot came bounding across the sky, Icarus became intoxicated with his powers. Instead of keeping to the straight and middle way, he flew higher and higher towards the sun. And so, alas, the wax melted in his wings, and he plunged down, down to the waters below, and drowned before his father's eyes.

Chapter Twenty-Two

Death

The winter months gave way to summer. One day in May, as Alexander was being taken by boat out among the marshlands and waterways north of Babylon, where there were many royal and ancient tombs, a sudden wind caught his hat and dropped it into the water. The royal hat blew away among the reed beds. This was seen as a worrying omen, but there was a further prophecy which stated that any man who wrongly wore the royal diadem must have his head cut off. Already, a Phoenician sailor had dived in to retrieve the hat and, when he found he couldn't return to the boat without getting the hat wet, he put it on his head and swam back.

Some say Alexander paid the man a talent then had his head cut off, others say he was simply flogged and others that he was paid his talent and not punished. But whatever the man's fate, the episode with the hat was seen as a portent, signifying Alexander's death.

Alexander returned to business, concerned to honour Hephaistion with temples and shrines. But soon came another portent.

While sitting on his gold throne, engaged in a meeting, Alexander felt thirsty. At that precise moment, he was unattended, so he got up from the throne to get himself a drink. Briefly, the throne was unguarded, except for the Persian eunuchs. From somewhere, no one knew where, a strange, deranged man appeared and sat down on it. Instead of throwing him off, the eunuchs began wailing and tearing their clothes, as this to them was a dreadful omen, suggesting something terrible was going to happen.

Although the man was hauled away and tortured to find out what had possessed him to commit such an act, he had no explanation.

A few days later, on 29 May, Alexander attended a feast in honour of his loyal general, Nearchus. Crowned admiral of a fleet, Nearchus was about to embark on a campaign to Arabia. Alexander went on to a late night drinking party with his friend, Medius, where Proteus, the nephew of Cleitus was present. There was some heavy drinking and much toasting of each other. Alexander raised his cup yet again, and drank. With a sharp cry of pain, he suddenly fell back onto his cushion. Saying he felt ill, he excused himself and took to his bed.

According to the royal diaries, a fever set in. For the next nine days Alexander tried to carry out his usual daily routines: he ate, slept, bathed, played dice, listened to stories, prayed and made his sacrifices, but the fever did not abate. He became too weak to walk and had to be carried on a stretcher. But still he continued to hold court and hand out instructions from his bed.

On 5 June, he was taken by boat to the summer palace of Nebuchadnezzar, thought to be a cooler place, but his fever continued and soon he was unable even to speak.

Desperately, his generals consulted the priests and oracles, and searched for omens for guidance. They remembered the words of Calanus, "I'll see you in Babylon."

Meanwhile, crowds were gathering. A boat had been seen going to and fro between the palaces. By 9 June, his officers had been told that Alexander was only ill, not dead, but now they were demanding proof, for all sorts of rumours had spread throughout the city. At last, the officers were given entry and, one by one dressed in their military uniforms, filed past his bed. Unable to speak, Alexander managed to raise his head to each one or signal his acknowledgement with his eyes.

One account says that Roxane was at his side, that he felt ill and, wanting to vomit, asked for a feather to tickle his throat. A feather was brought to him by Iollas, a secret enemy who had tipped it with poison, a special poison, which had been smuggled to Babylon from Athens in the hoof of an ass. One account states that on the night of 9 June, lying in his bedroom alone, he ordered the door that led down to the river Euphrates to be opened and sent away his guards.

One historian wrote:

It was midnight. Alexander rose from his bed. He snuffed out the candle then, crawling weakly on all fours, made for a door which led out to the river. Gasping with pain, he dragged himself down to the bank, determined to throw himself into the waters and disappear forever.

How much better to vanish like a god than die a weak, human death. But Roxane returned to the bedroom and, finding it empty, rushed out

to look for him. Hearing his groans, she followed them to the riverbank. She threw her arms around him, and begged him not to die, so he allowed her to lead him back to bed.

Roxane nursed him with drugs and remedies, but he was gripped by the final death throes. It was she who closed his eyes and kissed his mouth to catch his departing soul.

Whatever the truth, whether it was malaria fever, typhoid or deliberate poisoning; whether it was through too much alcohol or the effects of old wounds – he had sustained 21 wounds throughout his campaign – "Alexander, son of Philip, son of Zeus-Ammon, died in the 114th Olympiad, in the archonship of Hegesias at Athens, that being on 10 June 323 BC."

DEATH OF
ALEXANDER

He was thirty-two years and eight months old, he was King of Macedonia and all the Greek territories, he had journeyed over 20,000 miles, founded seventeen cities named Alexandria, had conquered all from the Danube to the Nile, from Greece to Egypt, Persia and India, and become Lord over Asia. He ruled for twelve years and eight months.

So, as the omens foretold, Alexander died in Babylon.

Alexander's body lay alone in the high hall of state, abandoned while the news sped to Athens. Conspiracies and power struggles swept through his officers and generals as they looked desperately for a new leader.

A terrible silence spread through the Hanging Gardens, over the walls and across the city. Everywhere was in darkness. It was as if the sun had been extinguished.

In Persia, a lamenting Queen Sisygambis starved herself to death.

He had wanted to be buried in his soul country, Egypt, and that's where he was finally taken. Not to the oasis at Siwa, where he had wanted to rest, but to his finest achievement, the city of Alexandria.

O Alexander, Iskander, Ishkander, Iskindar or Skander!

Should we rejoice at the death of a bloodthirsty conqueror, or mourn for the loss of a genius?

Did Alexander, looking down from his heavens as a god, or mortal soul, see how all his dreams and ambitions for a unified empire, stretching from Macedonia to India, fell apart so quickly? Did he despair, as others without his vision fought tooth and nail in deadly power struggles?

Remember, he had set off as a young man of 22, with fire in his belly, eager to be as heroic and famous a warrior as Achilles. But by the time he died, a mere twelve years later, his vision had extended. He had become more than just a conquering warrior; he was a builder, an explorer, a man who saw the potential for world trade; a man who, when he wasn't fighting and conquering, was seeing where routes by land and sea could be opened up, harbours built, marshes drained and cities governed based on the Greek concept of democracy. He was a man of education and curiosity, who loved the arts and philosophy, who had a vision of a vast interaction of peoples, cultures and goods being exchanged across his empire.

Had he lived to his sixties, as so many of his soldiers and generals did, what kind of world would we have inherited?

Yet wherever he did pass, his name lives on, written into histories, myth, legends, romances and folk tales.

ALEXANDER'S HAND

The Persian storytellers sing:

"Hear how Alexander conquered the east, the west, the north and the south — all belonged to him — he won the world, but lost his soul!"

When Alexander died, his weeping friends and officers placed his body in a coffin, but as they tried to close the lid, his hand thrust outwards. They tried to press it down and hold it shut again, but every time they pushed it back his hand flew out again.

"What are we to do? Alexander is dead, we have put our ear to his chest, and no heart beats, we have put our cheek to his mouth, but there is not one breath of air, and yet his hand will not stay down," his friends wailed.

All sorts of physicians and priests came to see if they could keep Alexander's hand in the coffin, but it kept stretching out as if trying to grasp something.

At last a wise old man came by. "I suggest you carry this coffin round the world, and maybe then, you will find someone who is able to tell you what to do."

So Alexander's friends carried his coffin from town to town until one day, they came to the town of Hegmatane, now known as Hamadan, which means "wise people".

The wise people of Hamadan came to ponder over the problem, but no one could find a solution. Alexander's hand kept reaching out of his coffin.

Just as his friends were preparing to move on, a strange, wild boy came over to the coffin. "Shoo, go away, boy!" They tried to chase him off.

But the boy said, "I know how to keep Alexander's hand inside the coffin."

At first they thought he was being cheeky, but when they saw his solemn face, and determined expression, they shrugged and said, "Well, what would you do, my lad!"

"Just pour a handful of soil into his palm," said the boy.

The men laughed at him, but the boy picked up a handful of soil and let it trickle into Alexander's outstretched hand. Immediately, the fist closed over the soil and the hand fell back into the coffin.

"How could that be?" asked the men, amazed. "Why did that work, and not the spells and magic and wisdom of priests? Where did this boy get such wisdom?"

"It is because your Alexander is still not done with conquering land. He wants more countries, more soil!" shouted the Persian boy.

EPILOGUE

Alexander had the beauty of a god, great power of strength and endurance, and a keen intelligence. He was not only brave, adventurous, and hungry for fame, but observed his religious duties faithfully.

Those who deem to belittle Alexander only reveal their own limitations. Any criticism should take into account his whole life and career. And if there is anyone mean and petty enough to malign Alexander, he should first compare himself with this "blackguard". He should confront the unparalleled global success of this great king, this undisputed ruler of two continents, whose name was known all over the earth, and then dare to open his mouth and abuse him. Perhaps he will finally see his own littleness, the triviality of his life, and the paucity of his own abilities.

ARRIAN: *THE CAMPAIGNS OF ALEXANDER*

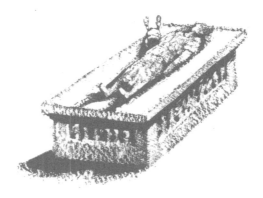

CHRONOLOGY

356 BC Alexander born at Pella to King Philip II of Macedonia and Queen Olympias.

340 Aged 16, Alexander quells uprising among the tribes of Thrace.

338 Alexander and Philip conquer Thebes in the battle of Chaeronea.

336 Pausanias assassinates King Philip, and Alexander becomes ruler of Macedonia.

334 Alexander wins the battle of Granicus. By winter, the southern regions of Asia Minor are under his control.

333 Alexander wins the battle of Issus. Darius III of Persia flees.

332 Tyre is defeated after a seven month siege.

331 Alexander founds the city port of Alexandria. His army goes on to win the battle of Gaugamela.

330 Alexander finds the body of Darius in an overturned wagon.

328 Alexander kills his lifelong friend Cleitus, after a quarrel.

327 Alexander marries Roxanne in Sogdiana.

326 Bucephalus dies, and Alexander founds a city called Bucephala.

325 Alexander and his army head into the Makran desert.

324 Hephaistion dies in Hamadan.

323 Alexander dies in Babylon.

INDEX

A

Abisares, Rajah 193
Achaeans, Harbour of the 37
Achilles 12, 14, 31, 33, 34-5, 137, 157, 200
   shield of 205
   tomb of 40
   and Troy 35, 36, 37, 40-4, 109
Aeneas 33
Aeschylus 14
Afrasiab 151, 159
Agamemnon, King 35, 36, 40, 109
Ahura Mazda (Persian god) 45, 156
Ajax 109
Alcmene 78
Alexander the Great
   and Achilles' armour 44
   appearance 13
   birth 12
   character 15, 172
   childhood and education 13-15
   death 222-30
   as the devil 102, 118-20
   marriage 175
   proclaimed king 21
Alexander's hand legend 229-30
Alexandria 96-8, 177, 179, 198, 225, 228
Amanian Gates 68
Amanus, Mount 68
Ambhi, rajah 190
the Ambrosial Rocks 81-3
Ammon
   Alexander as Zeus-Ammon 102, 111, 118, 177, 219
   Oracle of 98, 99-101
Amun 96
Anahita 55-6
Anubis 95
Aphrodite 56
Apis the Bull 88, 95-6
Apollo 56-7

Arad Ea 134, 136
Archaemenid Highway 33, 59
Aristander 30-1
Aristotle 15, 30, 36, 98, 152, 171, 177, 178, 198
Arjura 182, 183-4, 187, 188-9
Arsames 64
Artaxerxes III, Persian king 88, 96, 214
Artemis 12, 55, 219
   and Orion 56-7
Aruru 128-9
Assyria 59
Athena 54
Athens 22

B

Babylon 121-6, 127, 137, 144, 148
   Alexander's death in 222-5
   Alexander's return to 219-20
   Hanging Gardens of 122, 225
   road to 102-7
Babel, Tower of 122
Bactria 151, 154
Barsentes 148, 149
Bel Marduk 122-3
Belshazzar 122, 123, 125-6
Bessus 104, 148, 149, 151, 154, 167
birds 103-4
"Black" Cleitus 30, 53, 167-8, 217
Bucephala 198
Bucephalus (Alexander's horse) 15-18, 19, 32, 74, 111, 198
Byblos 77, 94

C

Calanus 191, 213-14, 224
Callisthenes 30, 152, 170, 171
Cappadocia 64
Chaeronea, Battle of 28, 29

Chiron 34-5, 79
Cicilia 64
Cilician Gates 64
Cleitus 30, 53, 167-8, 217, 223
Coenus 194-5, 200
Craterus 193, 194, 208, 209, 210
Cyrus the Great 13, 126, 144-5, 208
    tomb of 213

D
Daedalus 200-1
Daniel the Judean 123, 125-6
Darius I, Persian emperor 59, 141, 177-8
Darius III, Persian emperor 13, 21, 33, 45,
        53, 63-4, 147
    and Alexander 47
    and Babylon 102-3, 104-5, 106, 107,
        121
    and the battle of Gaugamela 108, 109-
        17
    and the battle of Issus 68-9, 70-7, 107
    daughters of 214
    death of 148-51
    and Miletus 57, 58
    offer of truce 86, 87
    and Susa 137
    in Syria 67-8
    and Troy 36, 37
    see also Persian army
Deianeira 79-80
Demaratus of Corinth 52
Demosthenes 21, 22, 152
Dionysus 12, 96, 166-8
    and India 177, 179, 180
Draupadi 185, 186-7, 189
Duryodhana 184

E
Egypt 33, 88-101, 102
    Alexandria 96-8, 228
    Oasis of Siwa 99-100, 102, 228
    Osiris and Isis 89-95
    Ptolemy as Pharaoh of 97

Enkidu 127, 129-32, 137
Ephesus
    Alexander's capture of 55-6, 57
    temple to Artemis 12, 55, 56
Euphrates River 105, 123
Euripides 14
Eurydice 19-20
Eurystheus 79
Eurytus 79

G
Gandara 177
Gates of Persia 140-1
Gaugamela, battle of 107, 108-18, 121
Gaza 86
Geryones, divine herd of 78, 79
Gilgamesh 127, 128-36, 137
Gordian Knot, the 60-3
Gordium 59-63
Gordius, legend of 60-1
Granicus, Battle of 46, 47-54, 57, 64
Greeks and Persians 46-7, 53-4, 141, 215

H
Halicarnassus 58-9
Hamadan 216
Hector, Prince of Troy 33, 34, 37, 41, 42
Hecuba, Queen of Troy 41
Hegmatane (Hamadan) 229-30
Helen of Troy 12, 33, 35, 40, 44
Hephaestus (the Divine Armourer) 42-3,
        220
Hephaistion 31, 40, 75, 117, 127, 137, 179,
        222
    death 217-19
    in India 190, 207, 208
    marriage 214
Hera 78-9, 167
Heracles 11, 12, 28, 96, 136, 157
    and India 177, 180
    twelve labours of 78-80
Herodotus 14
Hindu Kush 148, 154, 166, 181

Hiram, King 82-3
Homer 33
    Iliad 14, 19, 33, 40-4, 109
    Odyssey 33
Hormuz, Straits of 208, 210, 212
Horus 93, 94, 96
Hujir 160-2
Humbaba, King of Elam 128, 130
Hunor 24, 25-8

I
Icarus 200-1
India 33, 36, 44, 127, 166, 177-8, 181-202
    holy men 190-1, 201-2
    Jehlum 192-8, 201
    the Mahabharata 182-9, 207
    monsoon 191
    return from 203-212
    snakes 191-2
    Thar Desert 199
Indra, Lord of Heaven 181-2, 185
Indus River 190, 203, 207-8
Iole 79-80
Iollas 224
Iphigenia 109
Ishtar, Queen of Heaven 122, 128, 129,
    130-1, 136
Isis 89-95
Island of the Blessed 134-6
Issus 67, 68-9
    battle of 70-7, 107

J
Jehlum 192-8, 201

K
Karna 182-5, 187-9
Kauravas 183-9, 207
Krishna 181, 186, 187-8
Kunti 182-3, 184, 187

L
Leonidas 13

Lycomedes 35
Lydia 45, 59

M
Macedonian army 30-2
    Companion Cavalry 30-1, 54, 112,
      116, 117
    infantry 31
    retirement of ageing veterans 215-16
Maghdah, Rajah of 199
Magyar 24, 25-8
Mahabharata, the 182-9, 207
Makran Desert 208-10
Malloi tribe 204-7
Mazaeus 104, 105, 116, 121
Medius 223
Melkart 78, 82, 83, 86, 177
Memnon 47, 63
Midas 60-1
Miletus 57-8
Minos, King 220
Mithridates 52
Moon tree 201-2
Multan 204-7
Musas 127
Myriandrus 69

N
Nabarzanes 148, 149
Nearchus 209, 210, 212, 223
Nebuchadnezzar 122, 123, 124, 125, 223
Nereids 37
Nessus 79, 80
Nimrod 25, 27-8
Nysa, city of 178-80

O
Ocean of Death 132-4
Ochus 96
Odysseus 35, 109
Olympias (mother of Alexander) 12, 15,
    19-20, 21, 175
Opis 215

Orion 56-7
Osiris 89-95
Ousos 81-2
Oxathres 74
Oxyartes 172-3, 175

P
Pandavas 183-9, 207
Paris, prince of Troy 35, 40, 44
Parmenion 30, 52, 58, 65, 67, 86
    and the battle of Gaugamela 110, 112,
        113, 116
    and the Battle of Issus 71, 72-3
    death of 153
    and Persepolis 145
Pasagarde 148, 213
Patroclus 12, 14, 31, 40, 41-2, 43, 44, 137
Pattala 207-8
Pausanias 21
Pegasus 15
Peleus 34
Persepolis 103, 139, 140-5, 148, 167, 213
Perseus 99
Persian army 47, 48, 154
    bodyguard (the Immortals) 72, 73-4,
        112
    Scythian cavalry 24, 112, 113, 215
Persian customs 151-2
    proskynesis 168-71
Persian Empire 13, 32-3, 45-54
    Greeks and Persians 46-7, 53-4, 141,
        215
Pharos Lighthouse 97
Philip of Acarnania 65-6
Philip II, Macedonian king 12-13, 16, 18,
    19-21, 22, 32, 48, 167
    and Alexander as the son of Zeus 98,
        102
    and the battle of Chaeronea 28, 29
Philoctetes 80
Philotas 30, 153
Phrygians 59-60, 60-1
Pillar of Jonah 67, 68, 71

Plant of Life 132, 135, 136
Porus, Rajah 190, 191, 192, 193-8, 199
Poseidon 37, 109
Priam, King of Troy 41
Priene 57
Proteus 223
Ptolemy 30, 73, 97

R
Ra, Egyptian god 93, 95, 96
Rama, Prince 136
Ramayan 136
Rock of Sogdiana 172-3
Rostam of Pehliva 156, 157-65, 180
Rostram 151
Roxane 171, 173, 175, 179, 190, 198, 201,
    202, 215, 217, 224-5

S
Sakuni 185, 186
Samarkand 151, 155, 156-65
Sardis 57
Saum 156, 158, 159
Selene 15
Semiramis 208
Seth 89, 92, 93, 94-5
Seven Wonders of the World 97, 98, 122
Shamash 129, 134
Sidon 77
Siduri 134
Sirius 56, 57
Sisygambis, Persian Queen Mother 75, 77,
    117, 139, 175, 225
Siwa, Oasis of 99-100, 102, 228
Sogdiana 154, 167, 172-5
Sohrab 151, 156, 158-65
Solomon, King 83
Spitamenes 154
Sun tree 201-2
Surya the Sun God 181, 182, 184, 185, 187
Susa 103, 137-9, 148, 213, 214
Syria 67-8
Syrian Gates 68

T
Tahmineh 157-9, 165
Tammuz 122
Tarsus 64-5
Taxila 190, 191
Thapsacus 105
Thebes 28-9
Thetis 34, 35, 40, 42-3
Thrace 19, 20, 32, 33, 166
Tigris River 105-6, 123
Timoclea, Lady of 29
Tripolis 77
Troy 33, 35, 36-44, 109
Tyre 77, 78-87, 103
    and the Ambrosial Rocks 81-3
    and Heracles 78-80
    siege of 83-6
    Temple of Melkart 80-1
Tyrus 82

U
Uazit 93

Uruk, city of 128, 129, 132, 136
Utnapishtim 133, 134-6

W
Water of Life 127, 132, 135-6
The White Stag 25-9

X
Xerxes, Persian king 13, 141

Y
Yudhishtritha 185-6, 187

Z
Zal 156, 158, 159
Zeus 12, 56, 58, 78
    Alexander as son of 96, 98-101, 102,
        111, 177, 205
    Alexander as Zeus-Ammon 102, 111,
        118, 177, 219
    and Dionysus 167, 179
    and the Gordian Knot 61, 63

ACKNOWLEDGEMENTS

I trawled through many accounts of Alexander, numerous books of myth and legend, and even the Bible. But above all, I must pay tribute to Robin Lane Fox's *Alexander* and the ancient historian, Arrian, and his book *The Campaigns of Alexander*, which helped me so much in forming my own telling of the myths, history and times of Alexander the Great.